CONVERTS *or* DISCIPLES?

All scripture quotations, not otherwise indicated, are from The New King James Version: © 1982 by Thomas Nelson, Inc. Used by permission.

Printed in the United States of America

Published by
Word At Work Ministries, Inc.
P.O. Box 366 • Placentia, California 92871 • U.S.A.

wordatwork.org

ISBN 0-940252-04-X

CONVERTS *or* DISCIPLES?

A Prophetic Word to the American Church

by Al Houghton

Table of Contents

This book is dedicated to
Jonathan, Julie and Michael Houghton—
including their generation
with the commitment of Psalm 78:4–7

"We will not hide them from their children,
Telling to the generation to come the praises of the LORD,
And His strength and His wonderful works that He has done.

For He established a testimony in Jacob,
And appointed a law in Israel,
Which He commanded our fathers,
That they should make them known to their children;

That the generation to come might know them,
The children who would be born,
That they may arise and declare them to their children,

That they may set their hope in God,
And not forget the works of God,
But keep His commandments . . ."

Preface

The origin and core message of this book was born out of a principle in Romans 4:16,17:

> "Therefore it is of faith that it might be according to grace, so that the promise might be sure to all the seed, not only to those who are of the law, but also to those who are of the faith of Abraham, who is the father of us all (as it is written, 'I have made you a father of many nations') in the presence of Him whom he believed, even God, who gives life to the dead and calls those things which do not exist as though they did. . . ."

This book started with a phone call from Joe McIntyre, President of International Fellowship of Ministries. The Lord had spoken to him that I had a message for the Northwest. He had already scheduled a ministers' conference and was praying about which speakers to invite. I had already given the same dates to a church in Hawaii. Joe said, "Well, please pray about it because God said you had the message." That was interesting, because I had nothing. The Lord had not given me a specific prophetic word. I prayed about the message because after fifteen years I know Joe to be a man of integrity. I didn't have anything initially and then the Lord gave me a word out of Revelation 2:1–4 where Jesus addressed the Ephesian church.

It was really a message challenging the American church as Jesus challenged the Ephesian church. The Lord did have a word and I had to present it. The Pastor in Hawaii graciously agreed to re-schedule and I ministered this word at the conference. It was called into being out of an extended dry season. The American religious landscape consists of many churches whose spiritual condition parallels the political atmosphere of England prior to World War II. England had chosen a path of least resistance under the leadership of Neville Chamberlain. As Prime Minister, Chamberlain responded to Hitler's aggression with a policy of appeasement, which only encouraged the conquering of additional nations until Britain itself was assaulted.

It seems a spiritual world war is looming over freedom to preach and practice the gospel as we have known it. The forces of spiritual fascism in North America are promoting their agenda politically, while the church stands seemingly impotent and paralyzed. The church has the capability of rising to fight a war but many, like Chamberlain, have pursued the easier path. The church stands at the precipice of birthing perhaps the greatest outpouring of the Spirit that America has ever seen, but the preparation requires growing a generation of leaders which refuse the judicial threats of Acts 4. Supreme Court decisions on prayer, the Ten Commandments, and separation of church and state have been greeted by a generation ensconced in "abandonment theology." When the early church faced Supreme Court (Sanhedrin) prohibitions in Acts 4, they assembled agreeing together based on Scripture asking for a greater anointing to obey God rather than man. We'll either continue in "abandonment theology" or rise to the occasion giving voice to the spirit confronting a nation who desperately needs to return to its biblical roots. The church must stand and be the CHURCH again! To that end and purpose this message is dedicated!

Chapter 1

What Is a Disciple?

In Revelation 2:1–3 Jesus commends the church at Ephesus:

> "I know your works, your labor, your patience, and that you cannot bear those who are evil. And you have tested those who say they are apostles and are not, and have found them liars; and you have persevered and have patience, and have labored for My name's sake and have not become weary."

As I came to verse 4, what the Lord had against the Ephesian church faded and what He has against the American church emerged: "One thing I have against you, you have settled for making converts and have not gone on to make **disciples**."

So much of what was said to Ephesus could be said to a significant segment of the church in America.

The American church has a number of things for which it has done a very good job. There may be many areas that need improvement but those will likely fade as we address the core issue. The Lord said to me, "We have settled for making converts and not gone on to make disciples." What does that mean for the church and the nation now? What does it mean for the future? Have we sacrificed what God wants to do? Perhaps we are seeing the results lived out before us in these very days.

Matthew 28:18–20 records the Great Commission:

> "Then Jesus came and spoke to them, saying, 'All authority has been given to Me in heaven and on earth. Go therefore and make disciples of all the nations, baptizing them in the name of the Father and of the Son and of the Holy Spirit, teaching them to observe all things that I have commanded you; and lo, I am with you always, even to the end of the age.' Amen."

Jesus said "make disciples." He didn't say "make converts." There is a very distinct and dramatic difference. The Greek word for disciples is *math-ayt-yoo-o.* It means to walk with a mentor until we catch and imitate their actions in thought, word, and deed. What have we, as leaders, done to the American church? We have settled for making converts, and sometimes the actions of spiritual leaders are not even those of converts. In some instances, we do a marketing survey to discover what people want and then we give it to them and call it "church." That is *not* the Great Commission and never has been. The Great Commission only begins with getting people saved. It does not end there as many leaders have pretended!

Romans 10:9–10 says:

> ". . . that if you confess with your mouth the Lord Jesus and believe in your heart that God has raised Him from the dead, you will be saved. For with the heart one believes to righteousness, and with the mouth confession is made to salvation."

Salvation marks the beginning of discipleship. We must learn spiritual principles which govern our growth and development. As a Father, God brought us to birth for a very distinct purpose. He has a plan and a specific purpose for our contribution to the Kingdom. Certain spiritual principles help us attain God's goals and therefore are worth pursuing. Galatians 4:19–20 says:

> "My little children, for whom I labor in birth again until Christ is formed in you, I would like to be present with you now and to change my tone; for I have doubts about you."

Paul's goal in discipleship was Christ formed in each believer so that both their words and actions perfectly reflect the image of the One they worship.

The Hebrew concept of "discipleship" was that we actually walk with the mentor until we can respond just like the one who trained us in thought, word, and deed. When Christ is formed in us, thought, word, and deed leave no doubt as to who we serve, who we love, and who we worship. Thoughts lead to words which lead to actions and the actions confess to the world the essence of what we value demonstrating our worship to be true or false. Revelation 22:10–11 says:

> "And he said to me, 'Do not seal the words of the prophecy of this book, for the time is at hand. He who is unjust, let him be unjust **still;** he who is filthy, let him be filthy **still;** he who is righteous, let him be righteous **still;** he who is holy, let him be holy **still.**'"

The Weymouth translation in its footnote on "still" says this Greek word ". . . seems to denote development and crystallization of character. . . ."[1] In context we would add, "until it is apparent or there is no doubt about who we worship." Discipleship is the process by which we grow toward the goal of perfectly reflecting the God we have chosen to serve. Verse 11 says this process of growth and development, or assimilation of character, is constant for both believers and unbelievers. The reflection of who we worship increases until it can be readily and easily seen in the church or among unbelievers. Unbelievers become progressively more unjust and more filthy as time progresses until they perfectly reflect satan's nature to steal, kill, and destroy. What god do Muslims reflect when they produce children volunteering as suicide bombers and account for the great majority of terrorism worldwide? The church grows more righteous and more holy as we advance toward the end. There is a day approaching when it will be obvious who each individual worships because of their corresponding words and actions. A disciple is one whose thoughts, words, and deeds show Christ-likeness and reflect the character of the King! As we approach the end of the age, there are only two options for character development. We will increasingly reflect Christ or satan.

The process of discipleship
It is a life-long walk
Having to do with what you think
Your actions and your talk

Focusing on maturity
And character formation
Being formed a royal priest
A holy habitation

Jayne Houghton

Chapter 2

What Is the Goal of Discipleship?

Jesus not only commanded us to make disciples, He taught us all the essential ingredients by example. Matthew 18:1–3 says:

> "At that time the disciples came to Jesus, saying, 'Who then is greatest in the kingdom of heaven?' And Jesus called a little child to Him, set him in the midst of them, and said, 'Assuredly, I say to you, unless you are converted and become as little children, you will by no means enter the kingdom of heaven.'"

The goal of discipleship is to act like Jesus in thought, word, and deed. If a child can do it, we can do it. The conversion process is progressive from thought to word to action. The goal is growth in character through manifesting biblical principle. It involves a conversion others can see through our actions, based on the inner core values of who we worship.

What is interesting about this passage is that it shows us Jesus' thinking concerning the issue of discipling. He has already told the Twelve that their names are written in the Lamb's Book of Life, which in our terminology indicates they are "saved," they are "born again," but they still need the process of "conversion." "'. . . unless you are converted and become as little children, you will by no means enter the kingdom of heaven.'" Since they had already confessed Jesus, believing Him to be Messiah, their names were written in the Lamb's Book of Life. Therefore the "conversion" Jesus was talking about was obviously not "salvation." What was the "conversion" then? ***It had to be a "conversion" of character through the engrafted word.*** Jesus chose to daily subordinate His will to the revealed purposes of the Father. The disciples would have to embrace the same process. Making every thought, word, and deed obedient to the Holy Spirit is the essence of true worship. Those who embrace this process become more and more like Jesus while those who reject it become more and more like the devil.

Revelation chapters 7, 8, and 9 show a progression of seal and trumpet judgments that come on the earth in response to those who reject this process. Revelation 9:20–21 says

> "But the rest of mankind, who were not killed by these plagues, did not repent of the works of their hands, that they should not worship demons, and idols of gold, silver, brass, stone, and wood, which can neither see nor hear nor walk; and they did not repent of their murders or their sorceries or their sexual immorality or their thefts."

Successive and continuous judgments are commanded against man based on who we worship. The core issue is outlined in verse 20 which says:

> "But the rest of mankind, who were not killed by these plagues, did not repent of the works of their hands, that **they should not worship demons**, and **idols of gold**, **silver**. . . ."

The Greek word translated "worship" here is *pros-koo-neh-o* and it means to move toward or bow in reverence or act like a little puppy running to the master, kissing or licking his hand as a sign of obeisance. The goal of discipleship is to grow in understanding so that when thoughts become words and words become actions, we recognize who our actions honor, bridling the flesh and saving ourselves from demonic deception and imminent judgment. One difference between converts and disciples is that converts very often fail to recognize or discern whose hand they are kissing or the ultimate repercussions of their actions. Converts, through deception, can unknowingly yield worship to demons.

Discipleship in its purest form seeks to bring us into Christ-likeness so that when the enemy's temptations arise, we can make the same decisions Jesus made; even when the pressure is so great that our sweat turns to blood and we have to say, "if there be any other way, let this cup pass from me, nevertheless not my will but Yours be done." Is it any wonder that Jesus talked about this growth as a process of ***progressive successive conversion***. He was very clear when He told His disciples, "except you be converted you shall not enter the kingdom of heaven." They were born again. They believed with all their heart that Jesus was the Messiah. But they needed significant and multiple conversions of thought, word, and deed, without which they could never have achieved their spiritual destiny. It is no different for us. This process of discipleship in its normative experience is life-long. It is hard to ever say that we have "arrived." But what we can say is ". . . we press toward the mark of the upward call of God in Christ Jesus."

In Philippians chapter 3, we find Paul talking about moving toward the goal of Christ-likeness. He also imparts a primary principle of discipleship in Philippians 3:7 and 8 when he says:

> "But what things were gain to me, these I have counted loss for Christ. But indeed I also count all things loss for the excellence of the knowledge of Christ Jesus my Lord, for whom I have suffered the loss of all things, and count them as rubbish, that I may gain Christ. . . ."

Growth in discipleship depends on our willingness to re–appraise what we previously considered our own and as an act of will, pushing it over into the loss column as God opens our eyes and we pass from deception to discernment. Paul said he was willing to push everything he ever thought was a big plus into the minus column so that he could gain ". . . the excellence of the knowledge of Christ. . . ." Our willingness to embrace loss, to obey, becomes a foundation for growth in discipleship. The cross was the primary principle for Paul. Great gain (salvation) is the fruit of willingness to endure great loss. Jesus established a pattern. It is an eternal principle that cannot be changed. Paul says in verse 12:

> "Not that I have already attained, or am already perfected; but I press on, that I may lay hold of that for which Christ Jesus has also laid hold of me."

The Greek word translated "press" is *dee-o-ko*. It comes from the primary verb *dio* which means to flee and the base of *di-los* and *all-ak-on-is*. *Dee-o-ko* means to pursue by fleeing from one thing and moving toward another. How much are we willing to put our actions under God's microscope and flee the areas that are not pleasing to Him and press toward those that are, as if we are His deacons (one who attentively serves another). This is the essence of discipleship and God is quite willing to show us those areas if we are willing to ask Him and make the changes. The heart attitude that willingly embraces loss becomes the essence of discipleship.

Paul continues in the same chapter of Philippians by telling what happens to the people who are not willing to walk out this pattern. In verses 17–19 he says:

> "Brethren, join in following my example, and note those who so walk, as you have us for a pattern. For many walk, of whom I have told you often, and now tell you even weeping, that they are the enemies of the cross of Christ: whose end is destruction, whose god is their belly, and whose glory is in their shame—who set their mind on earthly things."

The issue of the cross is the issue of the willingness to count things loss, push them over to the minus column, and accept God's standard. Those who are not willing to do that, Paul says in verse 19, have an end. It is called destruction, because ". . . their god is their belly, their glory is in their shame. . . ." Actions demonstrate who we worship. Choosing loss and Christ-likeness demonstrates worship of Jesus. Choosing discipleship means choosing the cross. Refusing to change, rejecting loss, and pampering the flesh demonstrates worship of the enemy. The latter path rejects the cross and invites ultimate deception. In advanced stages, those refusing the cross are usually very proud of what they do and what they say when, in fact, it is the essence and foundation for their judgment because they ". . . set their *mind* on earthly things." Jesus said, ". . . a man's life does not consist of the abundance of things he possesses."

But what things were gain to me
Those I counted loss
That I may gain my Savior dear
And through Him bear my cross

Jayne Houghton

Chapter 3

Discipleship Determined by Historical Events

Jesus made discipleship spontaneous, relevant, and progressive. A good example is Matthew 16:13 where He says, "Who do men say that I, the Son of Man, am?" He initiates circumstances which will reveal their flesh and present another opportunity for "conversion." The target this time is going to be their belief about end-time events. He poses a question and demands an answer in verses 14–16:

> "So they said, 'Some say John the Baptist, some Elijah, and others Jeremiah or one of the prophets.' He said to them, 'But who do you say that I am?' And Simon Peter answered and said, 'You are the Christ, the Son of the living God.'"

Isn't it interesting how Peter gets the exact revelation and is then able to speak it forth. That was an "atta boy" moment for Peter, who did very well. But Jesus was after something else. The disciples were being set up. Jesus was pursuing this line because He was positioning them for the "transformation," for a "metamorphosis" or a paradigm shift in their thinking. Are we being positioned for a shift in what we are facing? It seems the greatest test of **discipleship** in my lifetime is upon the church.

The next step unfolds in verses 20–22:

> "Then He commanded His disciples that they should tell no one that He was Jesus the Christ. From that time Jesus began to show to His disciples that He must go to Jerusalem, and suffer many things from the elders and chief priests and scribes, and be killed, and be raised again the third day. Then Peter took Him aside and began to rebuke Him, saying, 'Far be it from You, Lord; this shall not happen to You!'"

Disciples grow to accept the Master's will when it is diametrically opposed to their own desires, while converts generally do not. Would we say that Peter, at this point, was a convert or a disciple? From the time Jesus called the Twelve **disciples,** it is obvious at many junctures they acted like the converts they were. Barriers to growth vary. What was their insurmountable barrier? The answer is their religious experience or theological mindset. Jesus said, "Your traditions make the word of God of none effect." The problem was in the area of what they believed. What they had been taught was not entirely accurate and they needed a conversion of thought. Peter had one mindset concerning the Messiah. He was coming to transform the government and make the Jewish nation the leader of the world. Peter needed a "conversion." Perhaps we should realize that those of us in the American church who are expecting **"the rapture any day"** may need the same kind of "conversion" that Peter did. What if persecution is coming and we have to pay the price to birth a new heavens and a new earth?

Peter needed "conversion" because of his eschatology. The prophetic emphasis on the Messiah as Judge of all the earth became a barrier masking recognition of the "suffering Servant." Is our prophetic emphasis masking our recognition? Is it possible that we need the same kind of "conversion" in the same area? Verse 23 says:

> "But He turned and said to Peter, 'Get behind Me, Satan! You are an offense to Me, for you are not mindful of the things of God, but the things of men.'"

How many of us in the church-world do the very same thing that Peter did but in a different way? How many of us because of the things we do, say, stand for, or align ourselves with become an offense to God because we are "***not*** **mindful** of the things of God"? The degree to which we are ***not*** **mindful** is a discipleship failure!

Precept on precept
And line upon line
True growth demands change
One step at a time

Each line takes you higher
Each precept more deep
A transforming unfolds
As God's ways you keep

Thus precept on precept
And line after line
Discipling happens
One truth at a time

Jayne Houghton

Chapter 4

Disclipeship's Lifetime Purpose

In John 21:18, 19 Jesus drew the ultimate distinction between being a convert and a disciple to help Peter over the hill into fulfillment:

> "'Most assuredly, I say to you, when you were younger, you girded yourself and walked where you wished; but when you are old, you will stretch out your hands, and another will gird you and carry you where you do not wish,' This He spoke signifying by what death he would glorify God. And when He had spoken this, He said to him, 'Follow Me.'"

The true essence of a **convert** is defined right here. In Christian youth we can walk where we want. We can *go wherever* we want to go. We can *do whatever* feels good. We can *give wherever* we wish, *go to church wherever* we desire, *show up* when we feel like it and *do whatever* we want, because "we" are the center of our universe. A disciple has a far different walk. We personally choose to be dethroned and voluntarily choose to enthrone the Holy Spirit in our decision making. Being a disciple means that when we wake up in the morning our life does not belong to us. It belongs to God and we place His purpose and priority as being preeminent.

Discipleship means being willing to go where God wants us even if it is going to cost us our life. Jesus was making that point to Peter. This is what the early church modeled. Peter accepted it. He said he was not worthy to be crucified right side up but demanded they crucify him upside down. Paul modeled this measure of discipleship. So did the Twelve. The entire early church modeled this dimension of discipleship. What dimension of commitment has been achieved in the Chinese church, Egyptian church, Canadian church, and finally American church? The question becomes, Are we going to rise to the level of previous generations in our commitment and our dedication to God's plan? If we don't, we may well lose a nation as well as a great harvest that has been prophetically promised. Jesus made it very clear to Peter that his death was not going to be what he wanted. He ended the encounter by saying, "Follow Me!"

True discipleship means following the direction of the Holy Spirit often when it is uncomfortable and totally against what we would like to do in the natural. "Follow Me" is the consummate call to discipleship where the end result is we are not our own. We recognize we have been bought with a price and we choose to fully yield ourselves to the One who has bought us, allowing Him to spend us as change in His pocket. Jesus said another will "carry you" where you do not wish to go. Are we seeing a generation with that commitment who are willing to go as evangelists into Islamic countries where they will most likely be martyred? This is the true test of discipleship. We cannot raise a spiritual generation to anything less. How can we raise any generation to this level if we haven't gone there ourselves? It is biblically impossible to disciple somebody beyond where we have personally gone.

Second Peter 3:10–13 outlines a major barrier to discipleship:

> "But the day of the Lord will come as a thief in the night, in which the heavens will pass away with a great noise, and the elements will melt with fervent heat; both the earth and the works that are in it will be burned up. Therefore, since all these things will be dissolved, what manner of persons ought you to be in holy conduct and godliness, looking for and hastening the coming of the day of God, because of which the heavens will be dissolved being on fire, and the elements will melt with fervent heat? Nevertheless we, according to His promise, look for new heavens and a new earth in which righteousness dwells."

When we look at the "Left Behind" series, we have to ask ourselves, Why has it sold over 62 million copies and continues to accelerate? Is there an appeal other than a biblical foundation, good fiction, interesting characters, and a good story? What makes the "Left Behind" series so appealing? We have to applaud the series and its impact on evangelism. It is certainly a great gift we can all give to our unbelieving friends. Is the underlying appeal one that would much more fit converts than disciples? Qualifying for the rapture and escaping the ensuing persecution has universal appeal. Only the unbelievers, at the time of the rapture, are "left behind." Their conversion and attempts to survive the Tribulation form the foundation for the plot. This could qualify as a **cross-less** message for the church unless the reader loses himself in the fiction and identifies with the characters facing persecution. There is no price paid in persecution except for the ones that are "left behind." The believers who are raptured at the beginning of the book miss all the trouble and tribulation. We couldn't preach that to Christians who have been and are being slaughtered in Muslim countries. We couldn't preach that to the church in China. The church in China wouldn't buy the series. Would it be as popular in a nation where the level of discipleship rises to martyrdom? The church in Islamic countries may wonder why they have the persecution but missed the rapture. When the culture and persecution demands discipleship rise to the level of martyrdom, how could we relate to a rapture? There really are only a couple of cultures in which such a hypothesis would seem plausible. **Cross-less Christianity** has greater sales value in countries where there is no persecution. The story should have much greater appeal to converts. **Disciples** see through it and are not moved by the fiction. It's a great series. It's entertaining reading. It's doing a good work evangelistically and should be enthusiastically supported for that reason. I'm personally for the series and support it as an evangelistic tool. If we remember we're buying fiction, then the series can be a blessing.

How many Christians will get their end-time theology out of "Left Behind" books? Will they be prepared if they have to face a decision to renounce Christ or die? Will they be prepared for persecution? Some of them might, allowing for faith accidents. Let's look at why this series is so popular. There is a discernment that is developed for disciples in the end-times that converts just don't have. It centers around the issue of persecution. It centers around a core-value of discipleship: allowing God to take us where we do not want to go. Where do we stand on this principle? Jesus outlined it to Peter as absolutely imperative, if he was going to finish his race in obedience! Jesus had to confront Peter, James, and John over the issue of what they believed about the end-times. Their belief actually made them hostile to God's work and purpose. We do not want to find ourselves in a place where our attitude parallels Peter's words in Matthew 16:22. What Peter had been taught prophetically became the foundation for resisting God. Are we living there and don't recognize it?

We are told by Peter that we can hasten the coming of the Lord. How can we "hasten" it? The issue of how we can hasten it must be addressed. Peter can speak to this issue because he was confronted by Jesus. Peter says it's absolutely necessary that the church understand we can hasten the Lord's return. Our question is, How do we do that? The answer lies in the kind of discipleship program which produces graduates whose life is not their own and who yield to being taken where they do not want to go! Moses' generation could have hastened God's work by rejecting the discouraging report about the giants. What needs to change in the American church to produce this level of discipleship?

Most of us know little or nothing of persecution. We have not had to walk into the face of it, but it is obviously coming. Commitment, dedication, and all the essential elements of foundational Christianity were settled at conversion and baptism in the early church. This pattern is emerging in an increasing number of nations. They understood *immediately* what the price was. The potential price for them was martyrdom. They settled those issues in the beginning. It was part of the "conversion" package because of the trauma the church faced in those respective nations. Do Western nations have that trauma in the form of persecution? They don't have it yet, but it appears to be coming.

Who within you calls the shots
Who sits upon your throne
Does Your life belong to you
Or is it God's alone?

Jayne Houghton

Chapter 5

Discipleship 101

Preparing For Persecution

In Matthew 10:5–8 Jesus began the preparation for sending out the Twelve. This chapter provides the most complete survey of their training in the gospels.

> "These twelve Jesus sent out and commanded them, saying: 'Do not go into the way of the Gentiles, and do not enter a city of the Samaritans. But go rather to the lost sheep of the house of Israel. And as you go, preach, saying, "The kingdom of heaven is at hand." Heal the sick, cleanse the lepers, raise the dead, cast out demons. Freely you have received, freely give.'"

The anointing to heal, cleanse, raise the dead, and cast out demons at a consistent level which satisfies can manifest at any time. Jesus commanded where not to go before empowering them to go. If we haven't faithfully established the borders and boundaries so that people can discern the difference between the holy and the unholy, the casual and the profane, then how can we expect to have what Jesus promised at the next level of anointing? Moses crossed the boundaries at Meribah and his action was very costly, according to Numbers 20:7–13, depriving him of the next level in crossing Jordan to possess the Promised Land. While we understand all corporate outpourings and individual gifts manifest strictly by grace, maintaining a move once birthed often seems to depend on character. Mature Christ-like character emerges when biblical boundaries are embraced. If we establish those boundaries then we have a platform not only upon which to ask God for a move of the Spirit, but to maintain the anointing to heal, cleanse, raise the dead, and deliver. Until we embrace His boundaries, we don't have the covenantal character to maintain what is given. Obedience at the initial level paves the way for transition to the next one. All these things are written for our admonition upon whom the end of the world has come.

In the Great Commission, Jesus made some things very clear. He said, number one, "make disciples of all nations." Number two, "baptize them in the name of the Father and of the Son and of the Holy Spirit." Number three, "teach them to observe all things I have commanded you." Jesus made it clear that we have an obligation to teach according to the example He left. Are we making disciples by following His example? Many of us want the power without drawing the boundaries, but it would appear that God really has no obligation to honor a request from the platform of partial obedience. Saul lost his authority and position because he substituted partial obedience for full obedience. Jesus Christ is the same yesterday, today, and forever. Asking Him for the fullness of His covenantal anointing based on a foundation of partial obedience, has little merit. An affirmative answer from on High might hurt more than help. Discipleship has to follow the pattern.

In Matthew 10, verses 9–13, Jesus warned the disciples to beware:

> "Provide neither gold nor silver nor copper in your money belts, nor bag for your journey, nor two tunics, nor sandals, nor staffs; for a worker is worthy of his food. Now whatever city or town you enter, inquire who in it is worthy, and stay there till you go out. And when you go into a household, greet it. If the household is worthy, let your peace come upon it. But if it is not worthy, let your peace return to you."

If we violate this passage by establishing a ministerial milk-machine mentality, which does not preclude manipulating for money, then the spirit of mammon will prevail and we will forfeit the anointing Jesus promised. In verses 14 and 15 the "sent ones" were to become a financial dividing line wherever they went. How the people treated the apostles determined how God treated the people. There is no obligation for God to make us a dividing line if we don't follow the pattern. One of the essential elements of the very first covenant God established with Abram was that He would bless those who blessed Abram and those who cursed Abram, God would curse, meaning Abram became a walking yardstick by whom others were measured. God measured—Abram did not. Abram became an awesome opportunity to every city and culture where he ventured. If they blessed him, God blessed them. If they turned their back on Abram, God turned His back on them. That is the covenantal position that ministries should occupy. We should be the opportunity of blessing for people when we come across their path. We forfeit that position by not maintaining integrity. There is a restoration coming for covenant principles as those of us in leadership choose the path of obedience. Barnabas became a yardstick by which Ananias and Sapphira were measured. God is establishing yardsticks in our generation but, like Ananias and Sapphira, many continue on toward destruction with no recognition.

In verses 16–20 Jesus begins to introduce the issue of persecution. Covenantal preparation is paramount. Not everyone can receive the message the disciples have been given. This passage says:

> "Behold, I send you out as sheep in the midst of wolves. Therefore be wise as serpents and harmless as doves. But beware of men, for they will deliver you up to councils and scourge you in their synagogues. And you will be brought before governors and kings for My sake, as a testimony to them and to the Gentiles. But when they deliver you up, do not worry about how or what you should speak. For it will be given to you in that hour what you should speak; for it is not you who speak, but the Spirit of your Father who speaks in you."

Jesus made it clear that when persecution arose, and they were delivered up to counsels, courts, and opposition, they were not to be concerned about what they were to speak because in that hour the Holy Spirit would give them exactly what to say. The perfect example of that promise was Stephen's defense in Acts 7. Are we preparing a generation to face what the early church faced? It was an essential part of Jesus' discipleship. Can we say that we have actually discipled people if we have not prepared them for persecution? I don't think we can say they have been discipled. Discipleship that has no preparation for persecution is not the discipleship Jesus displayed.

In verses 21-24 Jesus said:

> "Now brother will deliver up brother to death, and a father his child; and children will rise up against parents and cause them to be put to death. And you will be hated by all for My name's sake. But he who endures to the end will be saved. But when they persecute you in this city, flee to another. For assuredly, I say to

> you, you will not have gone through the cities of Israel before the Son of Man comes. A disciple is not above his teacher, nor a servant above his master."

Discipleship has to prepare people for betrayal, even within their own family. This is pretty strong and may be unthinkable for many who live in America. It's certainly not unthinkable if you live in China or in a Muslim country. What is the level of discipleship that we are extending today? Have we prepared those called to evangelize Muslims for capture and beheading? Will converts stand? If we have the opportunity to make disciples, but are afraid of offending them or losing their tithe money, how could we ever face Jesus? If persecution breaks out, will we be giving account to the Lord Himself for those people who couldn't stand because we allowed them to remain immature converts? Jesus refused to leave the Twelve in that condition. Do we see the difference? Have we prepared the next generation for rapture or have we prepared them for martyrdom! What yardstick have we built into the next generation?

Matthew 10:22–28 says:

> "And you will be hated by all for My name's sake. But he who endures to the end will be saved. But when they persecute you in this city, flee to another. For assuredly, I say to you, you will not have gone through the cities of Israel before the Son of Man comes. A disciple is not above his teacher, nor a servant above his master. It is enough for a disciple that he be like his teacher, and a servant like his master. If they have called the master of the house Beelzebub, how much more will they call those of his household! Therefore do not fear them. For there is nothing covered that will not be revealed, and hidden that will not be known. Whatever I tell you in the dark, speak in the light; and what you hear in the

ear, preach on the housetops. And do not fear those who kill the body but cannot kill the soul. But rather fear Him who is able to destroy both soul and body in hell."

This is the core passage, outlining initial discipleship instruction. After reading this, how can anybody say that we should not prepare a generation for martyrdom? How clear is it when Jesus said "a disciple is not above his teacher nor a servant above his master"? How defining is it when He says, in verse 28:

"And do not fear those who kill the body but cannot kill the soul. But rather fear Him who is able to destroy both soul and body in hell."

Is the fear of the Lord resident in the church today or do we freely go about our business without ever any thought of this principle? Perhaps reading the "Left Behind" series is very, very comforting for a believer. For an unbeliever it is fearful and consequently a wonderful witnessing tool. Will we be surprised if we face persecution like Jesus did? How will we respond? If we have embraced a theology that is **cross-less,** we are in trouble. How is the Christian church doing in Muslim nations? What will they say to us when we stand side by side in eternity? Is our witness as strong as theirs? Is our commitment parallel with theirs? Are we willing to stand with the underground church? How will we compare in eternity? Jesus made it obvious that He was going to prepare the disciples to face exactly what He faced. To do any less is to deny the biblical pattern and to endanger an entire generation.

Matthew 10:29–38 says:

"Are not two sparrows sold for a copper coin? And not one of them falls to the ground apart from your Father's will. But the

> very hairs of your head are all numbered. Do not fear therefore; you are of more value than many sparrows. Therefore whoever confesses Me before men, him I will also confess before My Father who is in heaven. But whoever denies Me before men, him I will also deny before My Father who is in heaven. Do not think that I came to bring peace on earth. I did not come to bring peace, but a sword. For I have come to 'set a man against his father, a daughter against her mother, and a daughter-in-law against her mother-in-law.' And 'a man's foe will be those of his own household.' He who loves father or mother more than Me is not worthy of Me. And he who loves son or daughter more than Me is not worthy of Me. And he who does not take his cross and follow after Me is not worthy of Me."

The issue of persecution is perhaps brought into greater view in verse 32. The preparation for it necessitates a platform in the individual by which he is empowered or enabled to follow the Lord in what he must say, whereas those unprepared probably can't. Verses 32 and 33 state:

> "Therefore whoever confesses Me before men, him I will also confess before My Father who is in heaven. But whoever denies Me before men, him I will also deny before My Father who is in heaven."

One of the things that should concern us at this juncture is the impact all the "rapture" teaching has had on the American church. I remember a couple of years ago receiving an e-mail from a friend relating a story told by a famous evangelist's brother about this church in a small town in Poland, during World War II. The Nazis rolled in to town and demanded everybody renounce Jesus and affirm Hitler. Because they had been taught the rapture and that God was going to deliver them, no one was prepared. The result was 96 out of 100 denied the Lord! Four out of 100 honored God by refusing to bow! The four were summarily executed. What fruit do we have when we do not prepare people for persecution and it suddenly breaks forth!? Have we made **disciples** or have we settled for making converts? In the tenth chapter of Matthew, 61 percent of the verses Jesus spoke concerning their preparation deal with persecution and martyrdom. I wonder how that compares with the percentage of what is preached in today's American pulpits?

After being with Jesus, how would the Twelve define discipleship? This is a question we must answer. Perhaps it would help to look at Paul's generation and his definition. What was the level of discipleship that Paul considered minimal to qualify? Unlike James and John, he wasn't there with Jesus. He had to get it through visitation, through study and prayer. Philippians 3:17–21 gives us a good clue:

> "Brethren, join in following my example, and note those who so walk, as you have us for a pattern. For many walk, of whom I have told you often, and now tell you even weeping, that they are the **enemies of the cross of Christ**: whose end is destruction, whose god is their belly, and whose glory is in their shame—who set their mind on earthly things. For our citizenship is in heaven, from which we also eagerly wait for the Savior, the Lord Jesus Christ, who will transform our lowly body that it may be conformed to His glorious body, according to the working by which He is able even to subdue all things to Himself."

It is obvious that Paul's definition of discipleship was Jesus. Anything less than the commitment that Jesus exemplified simply didn't meet the standard. The degree to which a person accepts the cross is the goal of discipleship. Anything less than 100 percent falls short. The core issue of the cross is the willingness to use our faith on our flesh and accept the will of God—walking it out day by day. Paul makes clear what happens to those who are not willing to embrace that standard. He called them "enemies of the cross of Christ" and he said their end "is destruction."

Paul made it quite evident in the book of Philippians what his yardstick for discipleship was. In Philippians 2:19–21, he said:

> "But I trust in the Lord Jesus to send Timothy to you shortly, that I also may be encouraged when I know your state. For I have no one like-minded, who will sincerely care for your state. For all seek their own, not the things which are of Christ Jesus."

The fruit of allowing people to stay converts and not moving on to discipleship is that they never get delivered from "seeking their own." And the conflict always comes between what is best for them versus embracing the standard that Jesus lived: "Greater love has no one than this, than to lay down one's life for his friends." How do I lay my life down day-by-day for others? Discipleship is the central command of the Great Commission. We were not commissioned to get people saved so they could go to church and do whatever they want to do. We were commissioned to make **disciples!** Disciples embrace God's will and will walk it out even if it includes their own death. They will walk out God's will to their own pain and hurt. How do we grow to that place? Does God have progressive keys that we can embrace that will lead us to such a level of commitment? How did Jesus take the disciples from the businesses they were involved in to the ultimate commitment they made at the end of their life?

That is a question worth exploring. The fruit of allowing people to stay converts is that "each one seeks his own." Mammon seems to be the major mistress maintaining this stronghold.

Will you step into the lion's den
When it means personal sacrifice
Or are you happy to stay in the gray
Where it is easy, comfy, and nice?

Jayne Houghton

Chapter 6

Depth of Discipleship — How We Use Our Faith

Everyone has been given a measure of faith. How we use it determines whether Jesus is routinely or occasionally seen through our actions. Jesus spoke to this issue in John 12:20–22 when He said:

> "Now there were certain Greeks among those who came up to worship at the feast. Then they came to Philip, who was from Bethsaida of Galilee, and asked him, saying, 'Sir, we wish to see Jesus.' Philip came and told Andrew; and in turn Andrew and Philip told Jesus."

The Greeks who came to Philip had one question, "Sir, we wish to see Jesus." Philip took it to Jesus and the next five verses answer how He can be seen in every generation. Verses 23–27 state:

> "But Jesus answered them, saying, 'The hour has come that the Son of Man should be glorified. Most assuredly, I say to you, unless a grain of wheat falls into the ground and dies, it remains alone; but if it dies, it produces much grain. He who loves his

> life will lose it, and he who hates his life in this world will keep it for eternal life. If anyone serves Me, let him follow Me; and where I am, there My servant will be also. If anyone serves Me, him My Father will honor. Now My soul is troubled, and what shall I say? "Father, save Me from this hour"? But for this purpose I came to this hour.'"

Jesus described the process of His own growth in discipleship that the Twelve would have to follow. The Seventy would also have to embrace this, as well as all who came after Him, if He was to be seen through the actions of His followers. Our own desires are the grain of wheat that have to fall into the ground and die. If we refuse, we remain alone. Verse 25 outlines the core principle:

> "He who loves his life will lose it, and he who hates his life in this world will keep it for eternal life."

The process by which we walk out verse 25 is seen in our daily determination of how we choose to use our God-given faith. To "love our life" means that we use our faith for everything we want personally, but to "hate our life" means we use our faith on our flesh to obey God whenever a conflict of interest arises. Hebrews 11 records Faith's Hall of Fame. They all have one major thing in common—they used their faith on their flesh, not to get what they wanted, not to make life easier; but they used their faith on their flesh to obey God! Perhaps Abraham would be a good one to look at because he became the "father of all them that believe." Abraham grew up in a patriarchal society. In his culture it was unthinkable to make any major move without submitting it to the patriarch for his approval and direction. When God spoke to Abram He said in Genesis 12:1:

"Get out of your country, From your kindred And from your father's house, To a land that I will show you."

It is obvious from the account in chapter 11, verse 31, that Abram submitted what he had heard to his earthly father:

"And Terah **took** his son Abram and his grandson Lot, the son of Haran, and his daughter-in-law Sarai, his son Abram's wife, and they went out with them from Ur of the Chaldeans to go to the land of Canaan; and they came to Haran and dwelt there."

Abram failed his first test but he didn't quit. He would have multiple opportunities until he learned how to use his faith to please God. It became a definite slow-growth process. After Terah died, in Genesis 12:4, Abram had another chance to use his faith on his flesh to obey God. Verse 4 says:

"So Abram departed as the LORD had spoken to him, and Lot went with him. And Abram was seventy-five years old when he departed from Haran."

God had told Abram to leave his kindred, but I'm sure it was a little scary to move to a place he had never been. Abandoning family must have been disgraceful in his culture. Abram still could not draw the commanded boundary. Once he arrived in Canaan there was a famine. Instead of staying as ordered, he decided to go south to Egypt. Each time Abram refused to use his faith on his flesh to obey, there was a price paid by his family. Sarai ended up in Pharaoh's house. Abram returned to the place of his departure and again had the opportunity to use his faith on his flesh. God helped him make the right choice through unbearable strife. Abram finally drew the boundary. Lot was given the first choice of direction.

Genesis 13:9:

> "Is not the whole land before you? Please separate from me. If you take the left, then I will go to the right; or, if you go to the right, then I will go to the left."

They were both herdsmen. They both knew the best land was the place that got the most water. Rainfall determined the pasture and the place of prosperity. Lot made his choice by using his faith for the prosperity of his flesh. The only problem was, the land was also defiled by the spirit of perversion, which would ultimately extract a tremendous price. Verse 11 tells us:

> "Then Lot chose **for himself** all the plain of Jordan, and Lot journeyed east [the choice of a convert.] And they separated from each other."

Here we see the difference in the two men. Abram was called to walk a path choosing the cross. He was called to use his faith on his flesh to obey God, and Lot was allowed to use his faith to try and advance his lot in life apart from the cross. There is the core difference. It is what divides the church today. The ultimate issue of discipleship is, How far will we go choosing the cross? Jesus continually used his faith on His flesh to obey all the way to death. We see the ultimate inner conflict over that issue in Gethsemane. Matthew 26:39 sums it up:

> ". . . Father, if it is possible, let this cup pass from Me, nevertheless not as I will, but as You will."

Abram would one day face the same inner conflict. His choice to use his faith on his flesh would earn him the gold standard of discipleship. A considerable amount of time passed after Lot and

Abram separated but he still had no children. In chapter 15, Abram was obviously frustrated because of unfulfilled promises and complained to God about having no heir. God came to him and gave him the blood covenant forming the foundation of the God-man relationship so that Abram might **know** what God had promised was guaranteed. Frustration continued to grow as long as God withheld giving him a son. A test came in chapter 16 with the carnal plan for children where Sarai suggested that Abram take her maid, Hagar. Abram's failure to use his faith on his flesh and obey God created more problems than he ever wanted. We are still dealing with those problems today since Hagar's son is the father of the tribes tendering terrorism. Sometimes when we don't use our faith on our flesh to obey God, we allow the creation of that which wars against God's purpose the remainder of our days and possibly beyond our days into succeeding generations.

Finally when Abram and Sarai were beyond child-bearing, an Angel came to visit declaring, "About this time next year, you'll have your son." At this point Abram pled for Ishmael, the fruit of his flesh. He tried to use his faith to persuade God to accept Ishmael. God refused. Within a year Isaac was born. Ishmael laughed. He mocked his younger brother during the weaning ceremony, and Sarah was offended. Ishmael and Hagar had to be sent away and Abram experienced tremendous grief. In chapter 22 he reached the pinnacle of his gifting and calling, becoming the "father of all them that believe." He used his faith on his flesh in an attempt to sacrifice and kill his own son at God's direction. God stopped him after he passed the test. Verse 12 of Genesis 22 records a personal pinnacle point of discipleship:

> "And He said, 'Do not lay your hand on the lad, or do anything to him; **for now I know** that you fear God, seeing you have not withheld your son, your only son, from Me.'"

How does God ***know*** that we really love Him, choose Him, and will follow Him all the way? The depth and degree we are willing to use our faith on our flesh to obey Him demonstrates to both men and angels our commitment and our discipleship. Jesus walked it all the way to the grave. We have to raise up a generation preparing them for the possibility of martyrdom. How can we lead the next generation into a commitment we have not made? Discipleship has a goal of Christ-likeness.

Another great example of the very same process, in Hebrew 11, is Moses. Moses grew up in Pharaoh's house. The taxing authority of Egypt filled his bank account. He was sought out socially. He had all the privilege, position, and fame that any society could offer. He had the best of the best! But when the time came he had a choice to make. He could use his faith to cover up his true heritage or he could use his faith on his flesh and give up all the blessing of Pharaoh's family and choose rather to suffer affliction with the people of God. Verses 24–25 of Hebrews 11 say:

> "By faith Moses, when he became of age, refused to be called the son of Pharaoh's daughter, choosing rather to suffer affliction with the people of God than to enjoy the passing pleasures of sin. . . ."

Does God expect us to use our faith on our flesh to overcome sin? He certainly does. It is called applying the cross. Moses did and others have done it throughout Scripture. We don't have any choice. We can either use our faith to protect our flesh or we can use our faith to obey God [the crucifixion is usually in the obedience]. How we use our faith determines what we hear in eternity, whether "I never knew you, depart from Me" or "Well done, good and faithful servant. . . ." Moses saw this principle because verse 26 says, "esteeming the reproach of Christ greater riches than the treasures in Egypt; for he looked to the reward." Moses used his faith on his flesh to obey because he saw the great reward. Verses 27–29 state:

> "By faith he forsook Egypt, not fearing the wrath of the king; for he endured as seeing Him who is invisible. By faith he kept the Passover and the sprinkling of blood, lest he who destroyed the firstborn should touch them. By faith they passed through the Red Sea as by dry land, whereas the Egyptians, attempting to do so, were drowned."

Moses used his faith on his flesh to give up the wealth of Egypt. Forty years later, after paying the price all those years, God honored his act of faith by giving the wealth of Egypt, not back to Moses, but to all those who he led out into the Promised Land. Everything he gave up came to the people when they spoiled the Egyptians. Walking through the Red Sea had to present an opportunity to use your faith on your flesh. What if the water rolled back over you while you were in the middle? The whole nation had to use their faith on their flesh to execute that command. When the Egyptians attempted it, they drowned. The judgment was complete. How can we teach a generation to use their faith on their flesh to this dimension if we are not willing to embrace it ourselves? We can only lead people as far into maturity as we have personally gone. There is a definite difference between the standard required for those of us who stand in the pulpit and those who sit in the pew. I've often been baffled by a passage concerning moving in the power of the Spirit that Jesus spoke in Matthew 7:21–23:

> "Not everyone who says to Me, 'Lord, Lord,' shall enter the kingdom of heaven, but he who does the will of My Father in heaven. Many will say to Me in that day, 'Lord, Lord, have we

> not prophesied in Your name, cast out demons in Your name, and done many wonders in Your name?' And then I will declare to them, 'I never knew you; depart from Me, you who practice lawlessness!'"

Lawlessness comes from the Greek word *an-om-ee-ah,* which comes from the root *an-om-os,* which includes the negative participle and the root. In effect this means practicing a principle that does not fit the pattern prescribed. What makes this unique is this passage includes qualified individuals who move in the power of the Spirit. They prophesied, they cast out demons, they did miracles. It would certainly seem that only believers can qualify to move in the power of the Holy Spirit. What principle did they miss that caused them to forfeit eternity? Did they use faith for the gifts but never on their flesh to obey? Practicing the wrong principle can be deadly. Will we preach the cross? Will we follow the biblical pattern? Preaching the cross as a Pastor has its own price—usually fewer people attending. How will we choose to use our faith? There is only one way to please God—faith! And the ultimate issue is how we use it.

Can you use your faith
on your flesh
To say “Yes” to God
and obey
Even though you don’t know
for sure
Circumstances will
go your way?

Jayne Houghton

Chapter 7

Mammon—The Major Mistress

In Luke 16:10–11 Jesus said:

> "He who is faithful in what is least is faithful also in much; and he who is unjust in what is least is unjust also in much. Therefore if you have not been faithful in the unrighteous mammon, who will commit to your trust the true riches?"

How we deal with money dictates the flow of the true riches that come from the Holy Spirit. It seems that in the realm of progressive discipleship, God starts with a commitment unto death and progressively applies that commitment in other areas. The dimension or degree to which we are able to follow Him toward obedience with our money determines how fast we move on to higher levels of discipleship where His true riches are dispensed. If we can't pass the initial test at the money level, then how can we handle true riches? This leads to even more questions. What are the initial money tests? What does Scripture mean by "true" riches? And **why would God use money for a dividing line**?

Luke 16:12 and 13 state:

> "And if you have not been faithful in what is another man's, who will give you what is your own? No servant can serve two masters; for either he will hate the one and love the other, or else he will be loyal to the one and despise the other. You cannot serve God and mammon."

How much of what is ours does God claim as His? Is there a point when the true riches actually become ours? Is there a sense in which we can dispense true riches in the form of healing or provision whenever we find somebody who needs them? The issue of whether we're going to serve God with our money or serve ourselves becomes the qualifier. Paul said he had no one else except Timothy for **"all seek their own."** Are we going to serve God with our money or are we going to serve ourselves? This seems to be a universal test. What we do with this test dictates the flow of the "true" and brings us to the core issue of why money is the dividing line. The answer to "why" is because satan has made it an issue of worship. We demonstrate where our heart is and who we really worship by what we do with **money.** It was the second temptation recorded by Luke and the last one by Matthew. In the last days, no one escapes this test. Can we stand before the Lord and say we have been obedient in all He has called us to do? Understanding the importance of money is necessary in order to move forward in discipleship. Does God direct us to follow a formula, or are we to allow the Holy Spirit to direct us in what we give?

The issue of money and worship have very deep roots. Ezekiel 28:13–14a points us to the earliest recorded origin of satan's existence and his job in heaven. It says:

> "You were in Eden, the garden of God; Every precious stone was your covering: The sardius, topaz, and diamond, Beryl, onyx,

> and jasper, Sapphire, turquoise, and emerald with gold. The workmanship of your timbrels and pipes Was prepared for you on the day you were created. You were the anointed cherub who covers. . . ."

Within his own body he had the ability to make music and lead worship. The worship leader of heaven was tempted and **the temptation of the worship leader of heaven was to do what *he* wanted with the worship *he* created.** This seems to form the essence of every mammon test. The question is, What are *we* doing with what we have been given? As long as we allow God to lead in our decisions, we are growing in discipleship. Lucifer didn't—and he lost his position! Discipleship has a very specific goal. The goal is reproducing the character and nature of Christ within every individual so that individually and corporately we can present Christ to the world. If He is not LORD *of* ALL, He is not Lord *at* all!

Isaiah 14:13–14 states:

> "For you have said in your heart: '**I will** ascend into heaven, **I will** exalt my throne above the stars of God; **I will** also sit on the mount of the congregation on the farthest sides of the north; **I will** ascend above the heights of the clouds, **I will** be like the Most High."

The trail he blazed was asserting ***his* will** over God's will, or becoming "god" over what he possessed. The initial mammon test is beginning to come into view. One of the things we have to recognize and accept is that what we have been given to possess is not totally ours to do with as we would like. God lays claim to some of it and He wants a **voice** in its distribution. Are we willing to give Him that **voice**? What if this is the primary issue? What if God is not nearly as concerned with where it goes or what we do with it as He is in the initial step of us giving Him the ***preeminent voice***? Does God direct what we do financially? If we can say what the Bible says in Deuteronomy 26:14b, "I have obeyed the **voice** of the Lord my God and done according to all that You have commanded me," then we are demonstrating ever-increasing dimensions of victorious discipleship.

This theme continues to unfold in Scripture. The issue of **worship** is far more important than many of us may have thought. In Second Thessalonians chapter 2 verses 3 and 4 we find:

> "Let no one deceive you by any means; for that Day will not come unless the falling away comes first, and the man of sin is revealed, the son of perdition, who opposes and exalts himself above all that is called God or that is worshiped, so that he sits as God in the temple of God, **showing himself** that he is God."

One of the things we discover about satan is he has to prove to himself that he is God. Notice the key part of verse 4 which says:

> ". . . who opposes and exalts himself above all that is called God or that is **worshiped,** so that he sits as God in the temple of God, showing himself that he is God."

The only way satan can show himself that he is God is to receive man's **worship.** The receiving of **worship** is the primary thing that proves (to the deceived) he is God. Without worship, he doesn't attain the goal. Somehow he must weave a web of deception, snaring people into unknowingly yielding worship. Mammon is a primary mode. That is why one of the initial tests of **discipleship** comes at this point. There is a pitched battle over it in the realm of the spirit and it must be discerned, it must be seen, and it must be understood.

The issue of who our actions **worship** is a golden thread that runs through the book of Revelation. Who we **worship** becomes the dividing line between those who believe and those who are deceived. In Revelation 4:9–11 we see:

> "Whenever the living creatures give glory and honor and thanks to Him who sits on the throne, who lives forever and ever, the twenty-four elders fall down before Him who sits on the throne and **worship** Him who lives forever and ever, and cast their crowns before the throne, saying: 'You are worthy, O Lord, To receive glory and honor and power; For You created all things, And by Your will they exist and were created.'"

When worship ascends to the Throne, it provokes an immediate response. **True worship** springing from obedient hearts impacts heaven. Satan is still jealous of God's worship. Once we recognize that, we can understand why the enemy is so driven to prove to himself that he is God through the avenue of worship. **True worship** comes when our words and actions reflect obedience to God's word and Holy Spirit guidance. When our words and actions, through deception, reflect obedience to an unholy spirit, satan receives that as worship and is empowered. What does that accomplish? It builds the kingdom of darkness. Is the battle raging for the worship of men? The answer to that is absolutely, **"Yes"!**

This battle for man's worship comes into clear view in Revelation. The first few chapters all present the theme of true worship in order that the counterfeit might be compared as we move toward the middle of the book. Chapter 5, verses 13 and 14 state:

> "And every creature which is in heaven and on the earth and under the earth and such as are in the sea, and all that are in them, I heard saying: 'Blessing and honor and glory and power Be to Him who sits on the throne, And to the Lamb, forever and ever!' Then the four living creatures said, 'Amen!' And the twenty-four elders fell down and worshiped Him who lives forever and ever."

The thread of worship continues through chapter 5. True worship enthrones God in the praises of His people, the consequence of which reflect a dramatic release into their lives as God begins to empower them.

Revelation 7:11–12 records true worship:

> "And all the angels stood around the throne and the elders and the four living creatures, and fell on their faces before the throne and worshiped God, saying: 'Amen! Blessing and glory and wisdom, Thanksgiving and honor and power and might, Be to our God forever and ever. Amen.'"

True worship continues not only as it comes from those who dwell on the earth, but also from those who are in heaven. Who we **worship** determines how we walk through this season of time described in Revelation. All of our actions have worship implications! When we are obedient to the leadership of the Holy Spirit, God receives that as worship and it magnifies Him. When we disobey the Holy Spirit, and yield to the temptations of the enemy, our actions are received as worship by satan. It is possible to worship the true God with our words and church attendance on Sunday morning but worship the enemy with our deeds the rest of the week. If this is happening to the church consistently, then we understand how the church could become impotent, having little or no impact on the nation, the Congress or the Courts.

Worldly longing for mammon
Can gain a death-grip
Away from your influence
The true riches slip

Who you worship is revealed
By what you do with the purse
Does your "money-obedience"
Bring a blessing or curse?

Jayne Houghton

Chapter 8

Fullness Demands Mature Disciples

The closer we get to the Second Coming of the Lord, seeing through the dark glass of biblical eschatology presents increasingly discernable images, making it easier to align ourselves with the principles that govern this transition. The transitional principle of **Fullness of iniquity** demands single-minded disciples, not fuzzy-thinking converts. Converts generally lack the commitment necessary to walk in the full measure of what is demanded in order to birth a new heavens and a new earth. As we survey the principle of fullness from Genesis to Revelation, that fact will become abundantly clear. Speaking of the length of captivity Israel would be in Egypt, God says in Genesis 15:14–16:

> "And also the nation whom they serve I will judge; afterward they shall come out with great possessions. Now as for you, you shall go to your fathers in peace; you shall be buried at a good old age. But in the fourth generation they shall return here, for the iniquity of the Amorites is not yet **complete/full**."

The Israelites were not allowed to possess the land of promise until the people who previously possessed it had filled the land with iniquity, forfeiting occupational authority. We know from Scripture that the "earth is the Lord's" and He assigns geographical areas to different people groups. Once assigned, no one can take the land unless its occupants fill it with iniquity. Once the iniquity of Canaan was **full,** the people who originally possessed it lost their divine lease and the land literally "vomited them out." The translation of "vomit them out" simply means they lost their ability to defend their territory, even if it was a good land, even if it was full of milk and honey. This principle continues in the New Testament and progresses into the book of Revelation.

Leviticus 20:1–24 outlines four specific spiritual principles, which, once violated, consistently fill a land with iniquity so the people can no longer defend it militarily. The first prohibition is the sacrifice of innocent blood. Statutorily protecting abortion fills a land with iniquity so the people can no longer defend it. Before the land started filling with iniquity, terrorist attacks were unthinkable. Since **9/11** terrorist attacks are expected. Why are we in this battle? One major root cause lays at the feet of the 1972 Supreme Court who decided *"Roe v Wade."* It lays at the feet of every judge who has struck down laws which have been passed limiting abortion. The blame belongs to every judge who has declared pornography "free speech." Muslim fundamentalists have called America "the Great Satan." Their illogical assessment has a component of righteous indignation in reaction to the public promotion of perversion. The perverse, filthy, and abominable decisions by our highest judges do ***not*** represent the majority of America. Muslims rightly object to pornography and homosexuality but carry no cure but the sword. Only Christians carry a cure with redemption! A war against terrorism ultimately lays at the feet of current Supreme Court Justices who continue to refuse godly wisdom, reversing partial-birth abortion bans by inventing and upholding the right to privacy. Under the banner of "equal protection," they have invalidated state sodomy laws and opened the door to the homosexual agenda. God does not extend equal protection to sin that destroys a nation. The sodomy laws were enacted when our forefathers believed Second Peter 2:4–8,

> "For if God did not spare the angels who sinned, but cast them down to hell and delivered them into chains of darkness, to be reserved for judgment; and did not spare the ancient world, but saved Noah, one of eight people, a preacher of righteousness, bringing in the flood of the world of the ungodly; and turning the cities of Sodom and Gomorrah into ashes, condemned them to destruction, making them an example to those who afterward would live ungodly; and delivered righteous Lot, who was oppressed with the filthy conduct of the wicked (for that righteous man, dwelling among them, tormented his righteous soul from day to day by seeing and hearing their lawless deeds)."

As long as our judges refuse to discriminate against sin, we can increasingly expect God's discrimination—judgment. Judgment comes to nations who were founded in biblical covenant but turn away from God! They are usually given into the hand of the enemies who summarily execute the evil doers.

The second principle filling a land with iniquity demanding a penalty is dial-a-demon psychic networks and the rise of occult New Age spiritualism. Leviticus 20:6–8 states,

> "And the person who turns after mediums and familiar spirits, to prostitute himself with them, I will set My face against that person and cut him off from his people. Sanctify yourselves therefore, and be holy, for I am the Lord your God. And you shall keep My statutes, and perform them: I am the Lord who sanctifies you."

Various forms of witchcraft pollute a land, causing people to lose their ability to defend it.

The third area is open rebellion against authority as outlined in verse 9.

> "For everyone who curses his father or his mother shall surely be put to death. He has cursed his father or his mother. His blood shall be upon him."

Probably in our generation, the most noted single cause of rebellion in the last fifty years has been the rise of the drug culture.

And finally the fourth spiritual prohibition is the statutory protection of sexual sin like homosexuality and lesbianism. Homosexual marriage and its equivalent, "civil unions," violate this spiritual law and, if judicially established under "equal protection," guarantee an increasing inability to defend our land. Verses 13,22–24 make that abundantly clear:

> "If a man lies with a male as he lies with a woman, both of them have committed an abomination. They shall surely be put to death. Their blood shall be upon them. . . . You shall therefore keep all My statutes and all My judgments, and perform them, that the land where I am bringing you to dwell may not **vomit you out**. And you shall not walk in the statutes of the nation which I am casting out before you; for they commit all these things, and therefore I abhor them. But I have said to you, 'You shall inherit their land, and I will give it to you to possess, a land flowing with milk and honey.' I am the LORD your God, who has separated you from the peoples."

The separation our forefathers embraced and statutorily encoded was not between church and state but between righteousness and unrighteousness. The generation which is witnessing the statutory repeal of barriers to sin is also witnessing the inability to defend the land, but apparently without any discernment concerning the true root cause. The church has been silent over this issue and it must be brought to the attention of the leadership of the land in the power of the Holy Spirit with covenant demonstration.

Every election we face as a church is a test of discipleship. Disciples understand they cannot, dare not, cast their vote in support of any politician, Independent, Republican or Democrat, who supports in any measure any one of these four avenues of defilement that cause the destruction of a nation. **Fullness** of iniquity is rising so rapidly in America that it seems increasingly impossible to defend the land. The issue is not whether we have a Democratic President or a Republican President. The issue for the church, and one we will have to answer is, Have we contributed to polluting and filling the land with iniquity with our votes? Revelation 14 makes it very clear that when Jesus returns He will destroy those who destroy the land. We better make sure we have not been a contributor to destroying the land by who and what we support.

Converts can get away with that because they don't know any better. Disciples cannot! If we have contributed to filling the land with iniquity, it is time we repent and change our ways ***now!*** This level of discipleship has to come to the church. One of the reasons that the Holy Spirit moved the early church out of Jerusalem is because Jerusalem became **full** of iniquity, and in A.D. 70 it was totally destroyed. The generation which filled the cup of iniquity under the Old Testament, by rejecting the very God they claimed to represent, lost what freedom to worship they had within forty years.

God's word works—not sometimes—not part of the time—but all the time.

Isaiah 28:11–18 records a prophetic word Isaiah delivered to the leaders at Jerusalem who scorned God's word and did their own thing. This word could just as easily have been spoken today to America's church and national leaders. The question we have to deal with in the church is, How much of what could be said to our political leadership really lays equally at our feet. Isaiah said:

> "For with stammering lips and another tongue He will speak to this people, To whom He said, 'This is the rest with which You may cause the weary to rest.' And, 'This is the refreshing': Yet they would not hear. But the word of the LORD was to them, 'Precept upon precept, precept upon precept, Line upon line, line upon line, Here a little, there a little,' That they might go and fall backward, and be broken And snared and caught. Therefore hear the word of the LORD, you scornful men, Who rule this people who are in Jerusalem, Because you have said, **'We have made a covenant with death, And with Sheol we are in agreement.** When the overflowing scourge passes through, It will not come to us, For we have made lies our refuge. And under falsehood we have hidden ourselves.' Therefore thus says the Lord GOD: 'Behold, I lay in Zion a stone for a foundation, A tried stone, a precious cornerstone, a sure foundation; Whoever believes will not act hastily. Also I will make justice the measuring line, And righteousness the plummet. The hail will sweep away the refuge of lies, and the waters will overflow the hiding place. Your covenant with death will be annulled, And your agreement with Sheol will not stand; When the overflowing scourge passes through. Then you will be trampled down by it."

The politicians who consistently support domestic partnerships or homosexual marriage are making a covenant with death. All who cast a vote for them participate in that covenant. The same is true for those politicians who support abortion. God promises to annul the covenant with death through judgment. How many cities will have to be devastated by terrorism or natural disasters until the church wakes up and takes a stand? Natural disasters can dwarf terrorism as the Asian tsunami proved. When sin causes the earth to convulse, disaster and devastation get redefined.

If gay marriage, by judicial fiat, is allowed to stand in America, three to five years from that final court case there will most likely be discrimination suits against churches in order to appropriate the property for the greedy and the perverse. The plan is to declare all opposition illegal through anti-discrimination hate-crime laws and shut down any contrary voices to a lifestyle that defiles a land filling it with iniquity. Don't think it can't happen here. On April 29, 2004, Canada's Governor General signed into law a bill which added sexual orientation as a protective category to that nation's "genocide and hate -crimes legislation." The legislation allowed ". . . the Bible to be deemed as 'Hate Literature' under the Criminal Code and in certain instances, as evidenced by the case of a Saskatchewan man fined by a provincial human-rights tribunal for taking out a newspaper ad with Scripture references to verses about homosexuality." The maximum sentence under this homosexual sponsored "hate-God" law is five years in prison.

Our forefathers criminalized homosexuality because they understood God's Word. To statutorily protect homosexuality meant incurring the discrimination of God called judgment resulting in the loss of ability to protect the land. Our forefathers were wise enough to choose to preserve the nation by statutorily discriminating against homosexuality. Today's citizens bent on rejecting God seem to desire to promote homosexuality and lose their land. The citizens of both Canada and America are finding themselves with a choice. Every Christian has the biblical obligation to love the individual caught in the sin while opposing the statutory promotion and protection of the lifestyle.

Jesus the Judge, in the book of Revelation, reveals exactly what He thinks of man's wisdom which is now surfacing in the refusal to call sin ***sin.*** Honoring homosexuality by statutorily protecting it guarantees God's discrimination resulting in the entire nation falling into judgment. The loss of freedom is the result. How could we dare think this is not New Testament when Jesus in Revelation brings seven seals, followed by seven trumpets and seven bowls. Those who try sleeping through the seals, or talking around the trumpets will bow at the bowls. By then it is too late for they've sealed their own fate. Many in North America want to spit in God's face and partake of the seals, trumpets, and bowls in full measure.

9/11 may well be just the beginning if we don't wake up and realize that God was not blowing smoke when He said we could fill the land with iniquity by statutorily protecting what He hates! It makes little difference what kind of laws the Canadian or American governments pass in order to promote the liberal agenda. The God of the Bible is **true** and we will witness and live through the progressive devastation of terrorism as long as our governments promote what God prohibits! Our ability to defend is diminished daily by a rush to legally protect and promote what God despises. The Bible tells us to love the sinner and hate the sin. Only in a Christian nation do people have the freedom to practice their sin in the hope that the goodness of God will bring them to repentance. How long do you think the homosexual would last in a Muslim nation? They would be footless, handless, and, quite soon, headless!

The Bible records God commanding His people to discriminate against sexual sin, including homosexuality, in order that they might have His blessing and keep their freedom and not lose it to other nations. God has NOT changed. Jesus said He did not come to change one jot or tittle of Scripture, but He came to fulfill it. He did! Those principles still operate today. History records the Roman Empire's descent into perversion and they quickly lost their freedom. It's a shame to be witnessing the same thing with North America. Every believer has an assignment to stand for the truth, proclaim the word of the Lord, and ask that God intervene. If the church remains in the immaturity of a convert we could lose our freedom. The season for disciples is upon us! The church has acted like its own worst enemy when attempting to influence the government toward godliness and away from iniquity.

It is certainly *impossible* to say *we believe* ". . . you cannot bear those who are evil" in Revelation 2:2, when we ordain homosexuals. I marvel that anyone with even the most cursory elementary knowledge of Scripture, let alone occupying the position of bishop, could actually sponsor and vote for such perverse behavior. Perhaps the answer lies on the other side of the coin. They probably know all the Scriptures about homosexuality but have educated themselves beyond their intellect and consequently have chosen not to believe what they read. When leaders abandon the Bible, it is time to abandon them. When a denomination has a significant number of bishops that can support the ordaining of homosexuals, the godly need to depart! The defilement of the altar is massive. Otherwise all those who give into that defiled altar open their families and their lives to the perverse spirit that the bishops have approved. How would you like to discover in eternity that you offered your children as a sacrifice to the spirit of homosexuality and lesbianism because you continued to attend and support an organization that ordained homosexual bishops?

If all we do is make converts and never teach the **absolutes of Scripture**, our flock is left to blow in the wind of deception on national issues. Whether or not to approve homosexual marriage is a momentous decision which legislates destruction on the land. How can a congregation act responsibly when the church ordains a homosexual bishop in violation of Scripture? Most converts know better! Filling a land with iniquity has the consequence of no longer being able to protect it with our military. Converts probably don't know enough Bible to understand the spiritual impact of certain public policy decisions. Discipleship should impart those truths.

The fruit of making converts and not going on to make disciples is that we continue as a nation to elect politicians and support political parties which absolutely promote wholesale national destruction and devastation. A discipleship failure enables people to unknowingly spit in God's face, ultimately resulting in judgment on the land! If church leaders would obey God, Christians would be voting with a clear conscience based on biblical principle. Why is our nation teetering on the precipice of major destruction? Because our churches are full of converts and not **disciples.** We're looking at the fruit of preachers pursuing success in the natural, based on numbers in attendance, while forfeiting success in the spirit. The men and women who will give account are the ones who stand in the pulpits of the land offering mush and milk-toast when they should feed meat. I would not want to walk into eternity in their shoes.

Nobody can say "I love God" and simultaneously covenantally identify with a politician who wants to establish homosexual marriage or the equivalent "civil unions"! Voting for a person is to become "one" with them. Attempting to serve God while supporting homosexuality is like having a spiritual split-personality of Dr. Jekyll and Mr. Hyde proportions. Why would anyone shoot himself in the foot? Yet people who claim to know Christ seem to do it consistently when they go to the polls. Jesus makes one thing clear. Just because we have recognized Him as Messiah doesn't mean we still don't have a tremendous amount of growth ahead of us!

Our culture is posing a question for the church, which has to be answered. Certain issues demand a response from every believer. When we go to the polls, choices are made which transcend political affiliation. If being a Democrat means supporting perversion, then temporarily stop being a Democrat. If being a Republican means voting for perversion, then temporarily stop being a Republican. By allowing believers to remain basic converts, we deliver them to deception, making a contribution to the demonic realm and bringing destruction and judgment on the land. Both priest and parishioner will have to give an account in eternity. Eternity is too late to say, "Sorry Lord, I didn't really understand the issues." At that point it is "loss-of-reward time." Discipleship is a front-burner issue. Why has the church backed off from discipleship? Are we afraid of losing people, or afraid of offending them and losing their support? It's time we got more afraid of offending God than offending man! There is a reason why American churches are full of converts and *not* full of disciples. The reasons lay right at the feet of those of us in ministry.

It is paramount to help people understand that a vote for abortion gives satan worship and is a vote to destroy the land and bring judgment on our own souls. To neglect this teaching is a discipleship failure. A vote to support political leaders who advocate "civil unions" is a vote to destroy the land, and according to Revelation, all participants will personally give an account to Jesus for it! Are we acting like converts or are we living like **disciples?** Are we converts needing "conversion"? Have we made political parties our idols and are we worshiping demons every time we cast a vote against God's principles? Do we lift our hands in worship every time we go to the polls and proclaim the praise of demons?

Jesus declared the price for elementary discipleship in Matthew 16:24:

> "Then Jesus said to His disciples, 'If anyone desires to come after Me, let him deny himself, and take up his cross, and follow Me.'"

Converts can get away with a do-what-you-like *phro-ney-o* attitude or mindset. The attitude is, "I can do whatever seems good." Voting for the political party of our youth can have a dramatic impact on our position in eternity. It can become an idol and cause us to worship at the altar of demons. It is necessary that in discipleship I face whatever idol has gained access and push it out! We've had a whole generation of leaders who have promulgated a theology of political abandonment and have totally left believers undiscipled, uninstructed and with no foundation for biblical decision-making. In most instances it is not the fault of the saints, **it is criminal neglect,** usually laid at the feet of ministers. The fruit of it is everywhere to be seen in America. We had best not make this mistake with the next generation or we'll all be changing our passports and looking for another nation in which to live, one which has freedom of religion.

Jesus summed up their discipleship in verses 25 and 26 of Matthew 16 when He said:

> "For whoever desires to save his life will lose it, and whoever loses his life for My sake will find it. For what is a man profited if he gains the whole world, and loses his own soul? Or what will a man give in exchange for his soul?"

What can a convert do that a disciple can't? A convert can fully follow his tradition, he can follow his flesh wherever it may lead. He is unaware of who his actions worship! But a **disciple** has to submit his actions to God through the word. Disciples ***know*** they have to yield to God. They have to bow the knee to biblical principle. When it comes to politics, the issue has nothing to do with the political parties, because oftentimes both candidates are incapable in their key policy positions of being supported biblically. The only ballot option in that case is to abstain. Which is more important to hear, "Well done, good and faithful servant," or "Thank you for voting the party line"? Isn't it time we got delivered from the idol of political parties and started the true process of biblical discipleship, where our choice on the **issues** reflects who we worship?

Learning obedience through discipleship ultimately impacts eternity. We have made such an emphasis on the formula for salvation in Romans 10, that we have neglected discipleship that determines our station and position in eternity. Jesus made it very clear that discipleship has a part to play in our growth and development in achieving eternity. Is our name written in the Lamb's Book of Life when we make Jesus LORD? Absolutely! All judgment and future reward depends on our growth in discipleship. We certainly don't want to suffer tremendous loss before the judgment seat of Christ. The only way to actively avoid that is to seek and grow as a disciple, submitting our decisions to the word of God! Converts become disciples as they choose God's word over every other influence! Fullness of Christ is the reward for the obedient while fullness of the enemy awaits all who continually yield to the flesh.

When we look at Matthew 23:32–36 we find that **fullness** was part of the transition from the Old Covenant to the New:

> "Fill up, then, the measure of your fathers' guilt. Serpents, brood of vipers! How can you escape the condemnation of hell? Therefore, indeed, I send you prophets, wise men, and scribes: some of them you will kill and crucify, and some of them you will scourge in your synagogues and persecute from city to city, that on you may come all the righteous blood shed on the earth, from the blood of righteous Abel to the blood of Zechariah, son of Berechiah, whom you murdered between the temple and the altar. Assuredly, I say to you, all these things will come upon this generation."

God established a new covenant when His people filled the old one with iniquity by killing the very One they claimed to represent and worship. Killing Jesus filled the cup with iniquity, according to His own prophetic proclamation in Matthew 23:32–36. **Fullness** governed the transition from the Old Covenant to the New.

Revelation 19:1–2 says:

> "After these things I heard a loud voice of a great multitude in heaven, saying, 'Alleluia! Salvation and glory and honor and power to the Lord our God! For true and righteous are His judgments, because He has judged the great harlot who corrupted the earth with her fornication; and He has avenged on her the **blood of His servants shed by her**.'"

We understand that fullness in Revelation 19 comes only one way. It comes when the old heavens and earth are filled with iniquity. It is the same pattern that brought the transition from the Old Covenant to the New. It's the same pattern that brought the Israelites into their Promised Land. Our New Testament promised land is a new heavens and a new earth in which righteousness dwells, according to Second Peter 3:13. The transition has to be birthed. This prophetic promise has to be bought and paid for, just like Jesus through martyrdom bought and paid for the transition from the Old Covenant to the New. Jesus is the Pattern Son. The question is, are we discipling a generation toward fullness that can pay that price and fulfill God's will like Jesus did, knowing it may cost them their lives?

How can we disciple people with a **cross-less, cost-less Christianity?** If we were discipled in cross-less Christianity, then it would be natural to perpetrate it on the next generation. We cannot afford to pass on the failures of those who parented us! Are we **disciples** or are we acting like converts? This thread of fullness runs through the book of Revelation. In Revelation 17:4–6 we're told:

> "The woman was arrayed in purple and scarlet, and adorned with gold and precious stones and pearls, having in her hand a golden cup **full** of abominations and the filthiness of her fornication. And on her forehead a name was written: MYSTERY, BABYLON THE GREAT, THE MOTHER OF HARLOTS AND OF THE ABOMINATIONS OF THE EARTH. And I saw the woman, drunk with the blood of the saints and with the blood of the martyrs of Jesus. And when I saw her, I marveled with great amazement."

Fullness of iniquity in the days ahead cannot happen without the blood of the church whose witness is rejected. Martyrdom is happening in a number of countries right now. It is not happening in many Western nations, but if it comes to America, will we have prepared a generation? Are we prepared personally? Will our children act like converts or disciples? They'll probably act just like us. How are we acting? Will they stand as Jesus stood—unto the death? Will they stand as the early church stood—unto death? Will they act like **disciples,** or will they act like converts who have never been given the intestinal fortitude to stand, because we would rather have a big church than speak God's truth to His people?

When the Communists took over China, the biggest problem in the church was betrayal. What we teach has fruit. Teaching the rapture as "prophetically imminent" creates great spiritual expectation. It totally anesthetizes the church against preparation for persecution. We marinate meat to change the flavor and tenderness. When the church is immersed in pre-trib rapture marinade, persecution reveals a flavor of betrayal. Those of us unaware of history may be doomed to repeat it! The church in China had not been prepared to stand! Many saved their own lives by betraying others. Are we building true covenant relationships where we go to church? The heart of the leader sets the agenda. Would we rather build something big, or would we rather prepare a people to face what is coming? One day we will answer for the leadership choices we are making.

Revelation 6:9–11 makes this principle clear and utterly indisputable:

> "When He opened the fifth seal, I saw under the altar the souls of those who had been slain for the word of God and for the testimony which they held. And they cried with a loud voice, saying, 'How long, O Lord, holy and true, until You judge and avenge our blood on those who dwell on the earth?' And a white robe was given to each of them; and it was said to them that they

should rest a little while longer, until both the number of their fellow servants and their brethren, who would be killed as they were, was **full/completed** [*play-ro-o*]."

What does it take to fill the old heavens and earth so we can get a new one? It takes the witness/*mar-too-ree-ah* of the saints. The word "completed" in the NKJ in verse 11 is the word *play-ro-o,* which means to fill the cup until no space remains. It is a verb. It demands action. God has already in mercy limited the number necessary to fill the cup. The question is, are we preparing any of them? Perhaps it is at this point we should consider another possible meaning of **9/11.** There is quite possibly a very strong message to be learned by the church. How is it that the followers of a demonized hate-filled philosophy have been discipled to the point of martyrdom so that they can bring destruction to one of the leading Christian nations in the world? Why have the deceived and demonized been better at discipleship than the church? Is **9/11** the partial fruit of an American church satisfied and complacent? If we had discipled the next generation of the American church would we have a large pool of empowered young people prepared to die for a Muslim harvest? The physical invasion of Iraq should have been immediately followed by a spiritual one. MacArthur asked for a spiritual army, promising Japan would become a Christian nation. The spiritual army never materialized and history records our eternally lost opportunity. If we take Psalm 2 seriously, asking for nations, then we must prepare for fulfillment.

Second Kings 6:8–12 says,

"Now the king of Syria was making war against Israel; and he took counsel with his servants, saying, 'My camp will be in such

> and such a place.' And the man of God sent to the king of Israel, saying, 'Beware that you do not pass this place, for the Syrians are coming down there.' Then the king of Israel sent someone to the place of which the man of God had told him. Thus he warned him, and he was watchful there, not just once or twice. Therefore the heart of the king of Syria was greatly troubled by this thing; and he called his servants and said to them, 'Will you not show me which of us is for the king of Israel?' And one of his servants said, 'None, my lord, O king; but Elisha, the prophet who is in Israel, tells the king of Israel the words that you speak in your bedroom.'"

God has an answer for Middle Eastern terrorism. Syria was very upset because every time they set a terrorist trap, Elisha alerted the king and Israel avoided the trap. The king of Syria believed there was a spy in his midst and finally had to be told by one of his servants that the real problem was a "prophet in Israel" who revealed every terrorist trap they set. We have a new covenant based on better promises. Where is this anointing in the church today which could avert future terrorist strikes? Are we behind, spiritually? Some politicians have blamed the government and its leaders for not doing enough on one hand, while on the other spiritually championing the very things that bring destruction. This blindness has to be exposed. It has to be rebuked. We need disciples. Disciples don't pop up automatically. They are made over a period of time. Are we behind spiritually? The answer is "yes." Do we have some spiritual ground to possess? The answer is "absolutely." Will God allow us to move into this dimension and save more lives, finally gaining a greater harvest? The word says He will. His word has the answer. That answer is in the anointing. But it has to be possessed. It is up to the church to produce the disciples capable of successfully traversing the end-times.

Are we discipling people into the realization of the price for walking out this end-time call?

Romans 11:12–14 says of the Jews:

> "Now if their fall is riches for the world, and their failure riches for the Gentiles, how much more their fullness! For I speak to you Gentiles; inasmuch as I am an apostle to the Gentiles, I magnify my ministry, if by any means I may provoke to jealousy those who are my flesh and save some of them."

Even the grafting in of the Jews is an issue of **fullness.** Paul realized that the church had to move in such authority as to provoke the Jew to jealousy to break the bands holding the disobedient and those who were contrary. We have a dramatic anointing to possess. **Fullness** not only governs the harvest of cities and nations, it also governs the grafting in of the physical Jew, and we in the church are responsible for birthing that anointing. In addition we're responsible to raise up a generation willing to pay the price to hasten a new heavens and a new earth.

Are we **discipling** people into the realization of the end-time preparational price? Are we discipling people into the prophetic depth necessary to possess a double anointing? Or are we selling them a **cross-less, cost-less Christianity?** What will it take to provoke the Jew to jealousy? It will surely be dramatic! Verses 25–27 state:

> "For I do not desire, brethren, that you should be ignorant of this mystery, lest you should be wise in your own opinion, that hardening in part has happened to Israel until the fullness of the Gentiles has come in. And so all Israel will be saved, as it is written: 'The Deliverer will come out of Zion, And He will turn

away ungodliness from Jacob; For this is My covenant with them, when I take away their sins.'"

Once again we see that the issue governing the harvest, whether it be Jew or Gentile or whether it be birthing a new heavens and new earth, **is fullness.** Are we going to walk it out? Are we willing to pay the price? What kind of fullness of anointing is it going to take to graft the Jew back in to the church? What kind of fullness is it going to take to birth a double anointing like Elisha walked in to avert terrorism and gain a greater harvest? Obviously this is not a season for converts. It is a time for **disciples.** The question is, Are we willing to embrace the ultimate level of surrender so we can walk others into it also?

Your vote is important
Just where do you stand
Are you in position
To defile the land

Is your intuition
And foundational belief
Based solid on Bible
Most solely and chief

Jayne Houghton

Chapter 9

How Did Jesus Disciple?

I hear Jesus saying to the church, ". . . you have settled for making converts and have not gone on to make disciples." The question which naturally arises is, How did Jesus disciple? Perhaps the best way to look at what He emphasized is to start with the Great Commission and then move back to the initial calling, preparation, and launching of the Twelve.

In Matthew 28:18–20 the Great Commission says:

> "Then Jesus came and spoke to them, saying, 'All authority has been given to Me in heaven and in earth. Go therefore and make disciples of all the nations, baptizing them in the name of the Father, and of the Son and of the Holy Spirit, teaching them to observe all things that I have commanded you; and lo, I am with you always, even to the end of the age.' Amen."

The word for disciples is *math-ayt-yoo-o*. It means to fully embrace your mentor until you can reproduce his responses in thought, word, and deed. It means to walk like, act like, talk like, think like, and work like the Master. Paul said to the Galatian church, "I labor or travail until Christ is formed in you." He also went on to say that he was afraid for their future. He saw a lack of maturity and growth, creating a vulnerability to be pulled back into deception and bondage of the law. Jesus had a goal for the church. Paul carried the same burden and was convinced it was his assignment to promulgate. His purpose was seeing Christ formed in every believer. That is the gold standard of discipleship. We cannot judge success by size or by the number of names we have on our mailing list, or the number of nations to which, as itinerant ministers, we have gone. Success in ministry has one standard. How much did we contribute to forming Christ in people? End of story! What would Jesus say about entertaining people to lure them into our congregations? What would He say about "feel good" programs that don't really impart the true stature of Jesus Christ? What would He say about the thousand and one gimmicks and programs created to increase attendance? Which is more important, attracting a greater number or ". . . laboring . . . until Christ is formed in every believer." Perhaps if we can get the goal straight then a move of the Spirit will follow.

Establishing Boundaries

Matthew 10:1–5 records the initial calling and sending of the Twelve. Verse 5 says:

> "These twelve Jesus sent out and commanded them, saying: 'Do not go into the way of the Gentiles, and do not enter a city of the Samaritans.'"

The very first thing Jesus outlined in the discipleship of the Twelve, before He sent them out, was what they could *not* do. He first established the boundaries that were out of bounds, in order to save them from wasting their time. He established clear direction.

He told them where *not* to go before He told them where *to* go. Perhaps one of the major problems we have today in our discipleship of people is we have not drawn clear boundaries; so, in many minds there are few prohibitions! We certainly haven't drawn boundaries helping congregations understand the principles that bring destruction based on the people we support at the polls. If we had been biblically discipling, the condition of the land would probably be a lot different than it is today. The current discipleship failure marks a whole generation. If America accepts homosexual marriage then we may be looking at the foundation for the beginning of the persecution of the church of which Revelation speaks. We find ourselves at a critical juncture in American church history concerning our future ability to impact nations. Will we rise and meet the biblical standard ordained or will we lose a harvest God intended us to have?

It may be time for those of us who are leaders to heed the Old Testament warnings in passages like Ezekiel 34:1–2:

> "And the word of the LORD came to me, saying, 'Son of man, prophesy against the shepherds of Israel, prophesy and say to them, "Thus says the Lord God to the shepherds: Woe to the shepherds of Israel who feed themselves! Should not the shepherds feed the flocks?"'"

Is it possible that the church leaders of Ezekiel's day faced the same pressures we endure today, such as not "ruffling feathers" when outlining God ordained boundaries? For the shepherds who did not establish the boundaries and feed the sheep, the word in verse 10 was quite harsh:

> "Thus says the Lord God: 'Behold, I am against the shepherds, and I will require My flock at their hand; I will cause them to

cease feeding the sheep, and the shepherds shall feed themselves no more; for I will deliver My flock from their mouths, that they may no longer be food for them.'"

Jeremiah is another prophet who saw a boundary problem and addressed it not among pastors but prophets. He said in chapter 23 verse 14:

"Also I have seen a horrible thing in the prophets of Jerusalem: They commit adultery and walk in lies; They also strengthen the hands of evildoers, So that no one turns back from his wickedness. All of them are like Sodom to Me. And her inhabitants like Gomorrah."

What was the problem with the prophets? Very simply, they did not draw the boundaries that God's word required and as a result people did not *know* what they could not do! Verses 21 and 22 state:

"I have not sent these prophets, yet they ran. I have not spoken to them, yet they prophesied. But if they had stood in My counsel, And had caused My people to hear My words, Then they would have turned them from their evil way And from the evil of their doings."

Real prophets confront sin nationally, corporately, and individually. People were unrestrained because the boundaries were neither taught nor delineated. They didn't realize the responsibility of what they were doing. God demands of leaders who stand before His people that we outline the biblical and spiritual boundaries necessary to stay in God's covenant. Those boundaries are honored or dishonored through covenantal representative alignments. They have an impact on most of what we do and how we conduct our lives. Any retreat from drawing those boundaries puts us in the category of what Jeremiah and Ezekiel saw and we become guilty.

Ezekiel 22:24–28 records God's rebuke for not establishing boundaries so people can understand, discern, and act accordingly:

> "Son of man, say to her; 'You are a land that is not cleansed or rained on in the day of indignation.' The conspiracy of her prophets in her midst is like a roaring lion tearing the prey; they have devoured people; they have taken treasure and precious things; [A prophet's conference where everyone is given a word can be a real blessing, but a prophet's conference where you have to pay for it by entering a hundred dollar line, five hundred dollar line, or have to buy a special wrist band entitling you to pathetic (I mean prophetic) ministry is another. The latter qualifies for this rebuke.] they have made many widows in her midst. Her priests have violated My law and profaned My holy things; they have not distinguished between the holy and unholy, nor have they made known the difference between the unclean and the clean; and they have hidden their eyes from My Sabbaths, so that I am profaned among them. Her princes in her midst are like wolves tearing the prey, to shed blood to destroy people, and to **get dishonest gain**. Her prophets plastered them with untempered mortar, seeing false visions, and divining lies for them, saying, 'Thus says the Lord God,' when the Lord had not spoken."

The issue was verse 26:

> "Her priests have violated My law and profaned My holy things; they have not distinguished between the holy and unholy, nor have they made known the difference between the unclean and

the clean; and they have hidden their eyes from My Sabbaths, so that I am profaned among them."

The meaning of this passage is very simple. The leadership did not draw boundaries and teach people to distinguish between what was right and what was wrong. They didn't cause them to grow. In New Testament terminology, we could say they left them in the simplicity of being a convert. They did not take them on to the realm of becoming a **disciple.** The consequences for the land were judgment and destruction. It seems we are facing a parallel situation today, possibly with the same result. What does God require of us as leaders?

Ezekiel 33:2–6 sums up the responsibility of leadership in such a season:

> "Son of man, speak to the children of your people, and say to them: 'When I bring the sword upon a land, and the people of the land take a man from their territory and make him their watchman, when he sees the sword coming upon the land, if he blows the trumpet and warns the people, then whoever hears the sound of the trumpet and does not take warning, if the sword comes and takes him away, his blood shall be on his own head. He heard the sound of the trumpet, but did not take warning; his blood shall be upon himself. But he who takes warning will save his life. But if the watchman sees the sword coming and does not blow the trumpet, and the people are not warned, and the sword comes and takes any person from among them, he is taken away in his iniquity; **but his blood I will require at the watchman's hand.**'"

How much blood will be required at our hands if we have not

faithfully established biblical boundaries that are obvious in Scripture?

Isaiah also prophesied about such a season as we face, when he said in chapter 28:16–18:

> "Therefore thus says the Lord God: 'Behold, I lay in Zion a stone for a foundation. A tried stone, a precious cornerstone, a sure foundation; Whoever believes will not act hastily. Also I will make justice the measuring line, and righteousness the plummet; The hail will sweep away the refuge of lies, And the waters will overflow the hiding place. Your **covenant with death** will be annulled, And your agreement with Sheol will not stand; When the overflowing scourge passes through, Then you will be trampled down by it."

How is it that we can make a covenant with death that God will annul? We can unfairly judge a leader's motive and begin a gossip/character assassination campaign undermining his authority. I've seen God annul those with a heavy hand. We can use our gifting to split a church and take part of the congregation starting our own work. God seems to have a special program for annulling those covenants. Perhaps the simplest way that church people make covenants with death today is they align themselves and support politicians who promote abortion on demand. They support politicians who push homosexual marriage, or "civil unions." Any politician who is for "civil unions" is also for homosexual marriage. Redefining homosexual marriage as a "civil union" does not confuse God! Politicians can't have it both ways. That little invention is engineered so they can say that they are against homosexual marriage, but support "civil unions." A "civil union" is giving homosexuals the same rights as married couples. It is nothing more than a semantic barrier in which politicians try to hide their perversion! Any person who votes for such a politician will find himself having made a covenant with death and God promises His judgment will flow to annul it! How many believers will be in that position because the boundaries were never drawn?!

I don't think any of us as leaders want to have to answer to Jesus for not teaching and establishing those boundaries. The very first thing Jesus did in discipleship was to teach them their boundaries—where *not* to go. The Bible is full of where *not* to go. Woe to us if we have not clearly enunciated those boundaries to our congregations. Observing the American church, we have to ask, Why do they act more like converts than like **disciples?** Who in the American church will allow God to take us where we do not want to go? A leader's discipleship can be no different than that of a believer. The same standard applies to both. Will we answer the call?

The Bible is full
Of where not to go
Woe to believers
Who don't read and know

The biblical boundaries
Are clearly spelled out . . .
Immerse in the truth
And stay on God's route!

Jayne Houghton

Chapter 10

The Redeeming Judgments of Revelation

Revelation 9:20–21 state:

> "But the rest of mankind, who were not killed by these plagues, did not repent of the works of their hands, **that they should not worship** demons, and idols of gold, silver, brass, stone, and wood, which can neither see nor hear nor walk; and they did not repent of their murders or their sorceries or their sexual immorality or their thefts."

These verses make it clear that the judgments of Revelation have a redeeming purpose. They are sent with one goal in mind. There is a reason why one-third of mankind is destroyed in verse 18 through the fire, the smoke, and the brimstone. Judgments come in an attempt to reach wayward men, creating adversity with the hope that they will stop the forms of demonic worship they are practicing. It is possible to say, "I love you, Lord" with our words, but set gold, silver, brass, stone, wood, and possessions ahead of God. Worship is more than what we *say*. It also includes what we *do* and the priorities we give certain things in life. If God's word does not occupy the top priority then we are assured that worship of the enemy is part of the mixture that has become our life. Demons receive worship through deception.

The sacrifice of innocent children is one of the highest forms of demon worship. It is received as worship by satan himself. While most in the church can say, "I would never do that," they consistently offer demons worship through deception. How could that happen? If, after singing hymns on Sunday and saying, "I love God with all my heart," we go to the polls on Tuesday and cast a vote for a candidate who supports and upholds partial-birth abortion, we have worshiped demons. When our politicians do everything they can to make sure that abortion-on-demand stays the law of the land, who is worshiped? Who receives **worship** on Tuesday when we cast a vote? There is great competition for our worship. And don't think worship doesn't have an impact in heaven! Our actions in worship impact both heaven and earth. Are we, who name ourselves believers, going to worship truly, or will we be caught in the enemy's deceptive devices, thereby making a covenant with death? Who is receiving worship when we go to the polls—God or satan?

In Romans 10:11–13 we are given God's prescription for salvation:

> "For the Scripture says, 'Whoever believes on Him will not be put to shame.' For there is no distinction between Jew and Greek, for the same Lord over all is rich to all who call upon Him. For 'whoever calls upon the name of the Lord shall be saved.'"

How is it that we can be very very familiar with what God requires for salvation, and find ourselves in the midst of a people who champion perversion under the guise of "civil rights"? That will *not* qualify as church but rather a gathering of political pimps masquerading as preachers. We have whole segments of our culture who go to church on Sunday and yet consistently promote what God calls an abomination and what the Bible says will absolutely destroy the land and bring a judgment on themselves, because they vote for those who statutorily protect that which fills the land with iniquity. And the result is that we can no longer protect it. Why is the church in America so grossly politically impotent? There can be only one answer. We have settled for making converts but we have not gone on to make **disciples.**

The American church consists of many converts, the majority of which don't know their right hand from their left concerning biblical principles, because they haven't been taught. That is criminal! But we are looking at the fruit of it. When Christian judges are blackballed by one party's senators, how dare we ever support that party. Any political party who supports "civil unions" or homosexual marriages is a walking spiritual death trap. This drama of choices made is playing out in our land. Isn't it time we made some changes and began the long, difficult road of **personal discipleship?** It's not enough to have major evangelistic crusades every year, because God didn't just say make converts. He said "make disciples." Are we going to continue our past historical pattern, or make the changes that are necessary to save and deliver a nation, one believer at a time?

Romans 12:1–2 says:

> "I beseech you therefore, brethren, by the mercies of God, that you present your bodies a living sacrifice, holy, acceptable to God, which is your reasonable service [worship]. And do not be conformed to this world, but be transformed by the renewing of

> your mind, that you may prove what is that good and acceptable and perfect will of God."

God's definition of our "reasonable worship" is presenting ourselves to Him that His word might shape us into the people He has called us to be. Ministers have the job of preparing the church for this challenge. If we are not in that preparational process, this verse says we have not offered "reasonable worship." Our initial conversion is to be followed by subsequent conversions as God's word becomes reality. "Making disciples" is a process mentioned in verse 2 of de-conforming to the world and transforming so that we are reformed into the image of Jesus. The Greek word used here is *met-am-or-fo-o*. It is a process by which worms become butterflies and it is a continual growth and transformation in discipleship.

In Revelation 11 we see the two witnesses come forth in such power that their testimony cannot be denied. In verses 15 and 16 we are told:

> "Then the seventh angel sounded: And there were loud voices in heaven, saying, 'The kingdoms of this world have become the kingdoms of our Lord and of His Christ, and He shall reign forever and ever!' And the twenty-four elders who sat before God on their thrones fell on their faces and worshiped God. . . ."

We find that true worship is the consistent theme that runs through Revelation bringing us even closer to God's ultimate judgment. God promises that He will overcome the enemy and He will reign in the last days; but when the judgment comes, where will we be? Will we be among the deceived? Will we have said with our *mouth*, "Lord, we love you with all of our heart" and yet with our *actions* given worship to the enemy? That is the real issue that is currently facing the church. We have to see the impact our actions have, and walk accordingly. If we don't, the fearful price paid will be eternity in the wrong place. We need to ask ourselves in all we do, which God will receive what I do as **worship?** The mentality that leaves Jesus in the church house Monday through Saturday is major league deception!

Revelation 13:11–12 says:

> "Then I saw another beast coming up out of the earth, and he had two horns like a lamb and spoke like a dragon. And he exercises all the authority of the first beast in his presence, and causes the earth and those who dwell in it to **worship** the first beast, whose deadly wound was healed."

We see, through counterfeit signs and wonders, the fulfillment of what is described in Second Thessalonians 2:3–4. The question is, how does satan do this? The ultimate in counterfeit signs and wonders duplicates the resurrection. That would be a lying sign and wonder because it leads people toward the worship of a counterfeit. Whether we interpret the book of Revelation literally or figuratively, the thread that runs through it is pretty clear. There is little doubt. The dividing issue is who will our actions **worship** as we walk through these end-times. When we start asking that question and applying the same yard stick to our actions, we are well on our way to guaranteeing being true worshipers.

Revelation 13:15–17 states:

> "He was granted power to give breath to the image of the beast, that the image of the beast should both speak and cause as many as would not **worship** the image of the beast to be killed. And

> he causes all, both small and great, rich and poor, free and slave, to receive a mark on their right hand or on their foreheads, and that no one may buy or sell except one who has the mark or the name of the beast, or the number of his name."

What is satan after and how far will he go to get it? Is the issue the mark? Is the issue mass destruction? The issue is **worship.** The enemy is willing to compel it by death. Are we preparing the church for seasons in which we either deny Jesus or are killed? Forfeiting our life is strong pressure to deny Jesus and worship another god. Are we preparing a generation for that level of commitment and dedication? Jesus prepared the Twelve for it. He told us to "make disciples." Are the disciples in American churches being prepared for this level of confrontation, for this level of end-time worship? Would we hear a message like this in most churches? Are we preparing people to worship the enemy if we don't bring them into this level of commitment? In our ministries, are we aiding the enemy by teaching people only what is comfortable and what they want to hear? Are we working for God or are we aiding the enemy? That is a question for all of us in full-time ministry.

Verses 6–7 and 11 say:

> "Then I saw another angel flying in the midst of heaven, having the everlasting gospel to preach to those who dwell on the earth—to every nation, tribe, tongue and people—saying with a loud voice, 'Fear God and give glory to Him, for the hour of His judgment has come; and **worship** Him who made heaven and earth, the sea and springs of water.'" . . . "And the smoke of their torment ascends forever and ever; and they have no rest day or night, who **worship** the beast and his image, and whoever receives the mark of his name."

Worship in the last days is determined by what we *do* and to whom our actions give allegiance, to whom we show honor. Worship is more than just what we say with our words. Satan has to prove to himself that he is God by getting people to worship him, and that means ultimately a generation will have to face death or denial of Christ. It's obvious that the golden thread of Revelation, whether we interpret it figuratively or literally, is, Who do we worship? As leaders, our job is to make the application *now,* preparing the church for persecution, even if we should catch the rapture. It is much better to be prepared to go through tribulation than to think we're going to miss it and suddenly find we were wrong. No generation can afford that. I don't know any minister who could afford to stand before Jesus and give an account for not preparing His people for what was coming. It is better to prepare and not need the preparation than to meet impossible circumstances having not been prepared. The blood of all who fail will be on the hands of those who did not make them ready. We should avoid that at all cost.

In Revelation 13:17 we're told:

> ". . . and that no one may buy or sell except one who has the mark or the name of the beast, or the number of his name."

The enemy's mark has its roots in **mammon**. Without this mammon mark, no one can either buy or sell. Throughout His three and one-half public years, Jesus drew a major distinction between His ministry and that of the Pharisees by declaring, "You cannot serve God and mammon." Mammon becomes a battleground for worship in the end-times. This process is further along than we might think. In Malachi 3:10–12 we find a very familiar passage:

> "'Bring all the tithes into the storehouse, That there may be food in My house; And prove Me now in this,' says the LORD of hosts,

'If I will not open for you the windows of heaven And pour out for you such blessing That there will not be room enough to receive it. And I will rebuke the devourer for your sakes, So that he will not destroy the fruit of your ground, Nor shall the vine fail to bear fruit for you in the field,' Says the LORD of hosts; And all nations will call you blessed, For you will be a delightful land.' Says the LORD of hosts."

Perhaps the first major mammon test that every believer faces is the issue of our giving. Are we going to submit to the Holy Spirit or are we going to make the same initial mistake which caused the worship leader of heaven to get kicked out? Who is Lord? Who will we worship? Are we lord over our money? Will we worship the enemy by elevating our own will? Or is Jesus Lord and will we submit spending to Him? We have to conclude that perhaps the reason this is the only place in the Bible where God challenges us to test Him is because the underlying issue is **true worship.** If we are willing to worship the one true God with our substance, then He says we can put Him to the test and watch what He will do for us. Mammon is a test every believer has to face. Would such a simple test ultimately lead to a valley of decision in Revelation where our ultimate destination is determined by that choice? Would any of us be able to say "No" to the enemy's mark had we not built a solid foundation through months and years of preparation? That is an interesting question that probably will only be answered the day we face it! Even if we don't see it, surely the wise among us prefer to prepare and understand our responsibility to warn the next generation.

In Second Corinthians 9:6–7 we're told:

"But this I say: He who sows sparingly will also reap sparingly, and he who sows bountifully will also reap bountifully. So let each one give as he purposes in his heart, not grudgingly or of necessity; for God loves a cheerful giver."

Giving, in the New Testament, has some unique underpinnings. They are not different from the Old, but they are certainly presented in a much different way, leading some to conclude that tithing is really not New Testament. They say the tithe would violate Second Corinthians 9:7, making giving "grudgingly and of necessity." That interpretation misses the point of the passage. Could we not just as easily interpret "So let each one give as he purposes in his heart" to be an issue of worship? If we give as we purpose in our heart, that is much more reflective of the issue of worship than fabricating some sort of compulsive declaration. The compulsive declaration argument completely misrepresents the whole picture of tithing as it is presented in Genesis all the way through to the New Testament.

Ephesians 2 says that we were "strangers from the covenants of promise" but "now . . . we have been made near by the blood of Christ." As we study tithing in its initial emergence in the Old Testament, the tithe was really brought to God as a covenantal blessing by both Abram and Jacob, which completely destroys the argument that in the New Testament it would be compulsory. It appears to me that it becomes our very first mammon test and the question is, Who are we worshiping? Those who say tithing is not mentioned in the New Testament are as blind as a goose in a snow storm. Exegesis is the science of biblical interpretation where we subscribe to conservative principles which allow the text to speak for itself rather than practicing isegesis, which is making the Bible say what we want it to! This destroys discipleship by making the text say only what agrees with our preconceived positions.

Genesis 28:18–22 says:

> "Then Jacob rose early in the morning, and took the stone that he had put at his head, set it up as a pillar, and poured oil on top of it. And he called the name of that place Bethel; but the name of that city had been Luz previously. Then Jacob made a vow, saying, 'If God will be with me, and keep me in this way that I am going, and give me bread to eat and clothing to put on, so that I come back to my father's house in peace, then the LORD shall be my God. And this stone which I have set as a pillar shall be God's house, and of all that You give me I will surely give a tenth to You.'"

While Abram is the one who initiates the tithe in Genesis 14, it is Jacob who voices the covenantal application of the tithe. It is Jacob who is asking for the covenant, not God commanding it! What we see in Malachi is the issue of **worship.** "Put Me to the test and see if I will not . . ." is God's response to truly worshiping Him by tithing. Jacob asks that he be kept in God's will with provision, clothing, and to be brought back in peace to his purpose for the establishing of God's house. The issue of our giving is an issue of **worship.** That's why it is personal and must proceed from relationship rather than from strict formulas. God must be allowed to direct. It is an issue of **worship and relationship.** The covenant blessings for tithing demand 10 percent be given. It is a covenant of promise. It is available and our choice of acting on it monthly is an issue of who we worship.

In First Corinthians 16:1–4 we find:

> "Now concerning the collection for the saints, as I have given orders to the churches of Galatia, so you must do also: On the first day of the week let each one of you lay something aside, storing up as he may prosper, that there be no collections when I

come. And when I come, whomever you approve by your letters I will send to bear your gift to Jerusalem. But if it is fitting that I go also, they will go with me."

What we see Paul doing here is saying Jerusalem needs help. One of the things they wanted to do was show love and appreciation for all Jerusalem had birthed. All the churches benefited from what Jerusalem brought forth. The gift was obviously Holy Spirit-motivated and Holy Spirit-received. When something is Holy Spirit-motivated, it can easily be Holy Spirit-received. Often, inner conflict comes when we are presented with challenges to give based on supposed "word of knowledge" or presented with an apparent need. The question is, Are we being Holy Spirit-motivated or demonically manipulated? The Lord is faithful to witness in those moments, whether it was God who originated the appeal, or man. The Holy Spirit will direct our participation. True worship results when we respond to the Holy Spirit, and if we don't get a Holy Spirit nudge there is no guilt, condemnation, or even shadow of concern in not giving. Only in following the Spirit do we become **true worshipers.** Following the Holy Spirit is our only defense against manipulators. Every believer must learn to give by "revealed need" not just "apparent need." Disciples give by revealed need while converts often give by apparent need.

Ephesians 2:11–13 states:

"Therefore remember that you, once Gentiles in the flesh—who were called Uncircumcision by what is called the Circumcision made in the flesh by hands—that at that time you were without Christ, being aliens from the commonwealth of Israel and strangers from the **covenants of promise,** having no hope and without

> God in the world. But now in Christ Jesus you who once were far off have been made near by the blood of Christ."

"Covenants of Promise" include the covenant of the tithe. While first initiated by Abram, it was later confirmed by Jacob. Jacob embraced and spoke this concept to God as if it would be a covenant. What he said was, "If You will do these things for me, then I will give a tenth to You." That is covenantal terminology. So what do we know about the tithe? It is a covenant of blessing. It is a covenant of promise and, as a covenant of promise, it is available to us for participation. As a result of participation in that covenant of promise, we learn true worship, and ultimately God insulates us from the counterfeit, deceptive, false end-time worship that we find in Revelation. Can we afford not to participate in this covenant? I don't think so.

In Genesis 14:17–20 we find the following historical account of Abram:

> "And the king of Sodom went out to meet him at the Valley of Shaveh (that is, the King's Valley), after his return from the defeat of Chedorlaomer and the kings who were with him. Then Melchizadek king of Salem brought out bread and wine; he was the priest of God Most High. And he blessed him and said: 'Blessed be Abram of God Most High, Possessor of heaven and earth; And blessed be God Most High, Who has delivered your enemies into your hand.' And he gave him a tithe of all."

It's hard to draw any conclusions from this passage because it is simply a historical statement of what happened. Abraham gained a victory and when God's priest met him to bless him, he attributed the victory to God. Abram gave him a tithe of everything he had repossessed. That is all we're told. The tithe doesn't really take shape as a covenant until we see Jacob's plea in Genesis 28. All the elements are here, but they are not stated in the way that we can conclude it is, in fact, a viable covenant. The essence is present, but a clear statement is not. God waits to define this covenant for us through Jacob in the third generation.

When the issue of covenantal blessing arises, Deuteronomy 8:18 presents us with a clear picture. It says:

> "And you shall remember the LORD your God, for it is He who gives you power to get wealth, that He may establish His covenant which He swore to your fathers, as it is this day."

Was Jacob asking for the power to get wealth? The answer appears to be "No," when we read Genesis 28:18–22. He was really asking God to bring him back in peace and to be with him, keep him in the way, give him bread to eat and clothing to put on. That is really all he was asking. He was asking for provision, not even substantial provision. But apparently because it became an issue of **worship,** God promised more than subsistence provision. I suppose we would have to explore the meanings of the word "wealth" and, of course, by New Testament standards that would mean our soul prospering, being in health, understanding the true wealth of God as much more than money. A man's life does not consist of the abundance of things he possesses. It is really His presence we seek in obtaining the salvation life, or "zoe" life that is in Christ. Deuteronomy declares we have a covenant of Promise. One aspect of this covenant in Deuteronomy is certain, the promise for finances to do whatever needs to be done. God appears to be adding emphasis as this subject moves through Scripture. He continues expanding our understanding so we can see how critical **true worship** is for every believer.

Deuteronomy 26 adds more understanding to the covenant promise of the tithe when it says, in verses 14 and 15:

> "I have not eaten any of it when in mourning, nor have I removed any of it for any unclean use, nor given any of it for the dead. I have obeyed the voice of the LORD my God, and have done according to all that You have commanded me. Look down from Your holy habitation, from heaven, and bless Your people Israel and the land which You have given us, just as You swore to our fathers, 'a land flowing with milk and honey.'"

This is what the people were to proclaim when they obeyed the voice of the LORD in their giving. It is obviously covenantal and it's obviously aimed at rewarding a people who truly worship God. The tithe has become an issue of obeying God's voice. It is a covenant that comes out of relationship which has as the core of that relationship —**worship.**

Verses 16–19 expand our understanding of this covenant:

> "This day the LORD your God commands you to observe these statutes and judgments; therefore you shall be careful to observe them with all your heart and with all your soul. Today you have **proclaimed** the LORD to be your God, and that you will walk in His ways and keep His statutes, His commandments, and His judgments, and that you will obey His voice. Also today the LORD has **proclaimed** you to be His special people, just as He has promised you, that you should keep all His commandments, and that He will set you high above all nations which He has made, in praise, in name, and in honor, and that you may be a holy people to the LORD your God just as He has spoken."

This passage promises that God in relationship through worship will meet the need that we present before Him. The Hebrew word translated "proclaimed" is a **hiphel causative verb** and it simply means that when we, in relationship and worship, ask Him what we're to sow, then we can covenantally declare, "I have obeyed the voice of the Lord my God," and know we can have what we ask Him. Our action of obedience to His voice causes Him to react toward us in covenant. When we say "Yes" to what God commands us to do in giving, then we cause Him to rise and agree to perform what we ask Him to do for us. This is the covenant. The essence of it comes out of **relationship.** It is formed and founded on the principle of worship. The tithe was never to be an arduous hard-to-perform command. It was a covenant of promise that was to come out of relationship in which God rewarded and blessed the true worshipers! Jesus affirmed it in Matthew 23 and Hebrews 7 where our High Priest still receives tithes today. Ephesians 2 proclaims the Covenants of Promise sure in Christ. How much more "New Testament" could tithing be?

I'm looking for people
Who desire to excel
For kingdom warriors
Who'll teach others as well

Who'll log kingdom miles
And not just be content
To walk in the "Sonshine"
And stay close to the tent

I'm looking for mentors
Who give selflessly
To impart to others
To invest faithfully

And such fruit amazing
Is the promised reward . . .
Will this be the purpose
That you're running toward?

Jayne Houghton

Chapter 11

Maturity in Receiving

If we, as believers, are to give based on relationship, those in the ministry are to receive based on relationship. Paul, in verses 4–6 of First Corinthians 9, says:

> "Do we have no right [*ex-oo-see-ah*] to eat and drink? Do we have no right [*ex-oo-see-ah*] to take along a believing wife, as do also the other apostles, the brothers of the Lord, and Cephas? Or is it only Barnabas and I who have no right [*ex-oo-see-ah*] to refrain from working?"

Paul is making a point about his relationship with God. He has chosen to conduct himself in such a way, in ministry, as to preserve his divine authority so that he can use it for advancing the Kingdom and helping people in the process. When we exhort believers to give out of their relationship, understand that the same principles operate in the ministry concerning the issue of receiving. That includes "when to," "where to," "how to," and the motivation or "in what spirit" we are doing it. Here is where discipleship gets really interesting. Can we **disciple** people into the depths of God in areas we have not gone ourselves? The answer to that should be obvious to even the most casual observer. There is a **greater** degree of discipleship required of ministers than there is of the Saints. If we're going to stand in the pulpit we have to stand there in the spirit of what we are teaching. If we don't, we hinder our congregation's growth.

In Luke 4:5–8, Jesus endures a mammon test. It says:

> "Then the devil, taking Him up on a high mountain, showed Him all the kingdoms of the world in a moment of time. And the devil said to Him, 'All this authority [*ex-oo-see-ah*] I will give You, and their glory; for this has been delivered to me, and I give it to whomever I wish. Therefore, if You will **worship** before me, all will be Yours.'"

When Jesus was tempted by the enemy we see that His temptation was a mammon test. All the kingdoms of the world, the gold, the silver, the cattle—everything was offered to Him as an *ex-oo-see-ah* **if** He would bow and **worship** at satan's feet. But God did not call Him to regain the lost authority *that* way. He was going to have to die and pay the ultimate price to regain it. What does that tell us about the connection between authority, mammon, and worship? They are directly connected. So in First Corinthians chapter 9, when Paul talks about his *ex-oo-see-ah* authority to partake of the offerings at the altar, and the Holy Spirit leading him to forego or refrain from that for a specific purpose, he is proclaiming the truth of discipleship, and living the example of using his faith on his flesh to obey!

How can we release the full divine covenantal authority for blessing the Saints when they give, and expect them to walk in relationship with the Lord *if* those of us occupying the pulpit are not fully yielded to the Spirit? The answer is obvious. We can't! If the church is stunted in its growth in this dimension, it is probably due to the historical tradition its leaders have set. When we stubbornly cling to tradition, we, like the children of Israel, forfeit our generational call and die in the wilderness of unfulfillment. Covenant is relational but when the issue in the church is money, we preach a formula (10 percent to the storehouse) as a substitute for relationship, because formula is more profitable.

In First Corinthians 9:11–14 Paul says:

> "If we have sown spiritual things for you, is it a great thing if we reap your material things? If others are partakers of this *ex-oo-see-ah* [right] over you, are we not even more? Nevertheless we have not used **this right** [*ex-oo-see-ah*], but endure all things lest we hinder the gospel of Christ. Do you not know that those who minister the holy things eat of the things of the temple, and those who serve at the altar partake of the offerings of the altar? Even so the Lord has commanded that those who preach the gospel should live from the gospel."

Why did God make Paul an example to the people "lest he hinder the gospel"? The reason was, all the others were using manipulation and every mammon technique possible to extort money under the guise of being led by the Holy Spirit. Paul found himself in the midst of significant financial corruption and he made a choice. It was a costly choice. He didn't always have every need met. He chose to walk another way. Paul was demonstrating the dimension of discipleship that is required of the priesthood, not of everybody—since there was only one Paul. But certainly this is a dimension that has to be addressed in the church. If we want restoration of apostolic authority for finances we must restore apostolic integrity. It is not optional. If we want the full power of the covenant, we must display apostolic purity.

Paul said in verses 15 through 18:

> "But I have used none of these things, nor have I written these things that it should be done so to me; for it would be better for me to die than that anyone should make my boasting void. For if I preach the gospel, I have nothing to boast of, for necessity is laid upon me; yes, woe is me if I do not preach the gospel! For if I do this willingly, I have a reward; but if against my will, I have been entrusted with a stewardship. What is my reward then? That when I preach the gospel, I may present the gospel of Christ **without charge**, that I may not abuse my authority [*ex-oo-see-ah*] in the gospel."

How is that for **discipleship** in action, obeying the Holy Spirit? He has the authority. He has the power, but he foregoes it to be an example that he may not cause reproach. Paul understands the dimension of abuse that most of us know is rampant in the church-world today. The spirit of mammon has a blood brother called manipulation. When ministers bow at the altar of manipulation, their divine authority is forfeited and the covenantal blessing on the people becomes a curse according to Malachi 2. Paul understood these weighty principles. It is time we began to believe for the full measure of discipleship to come forth in the church-world in the same measure of integrity in which Paul brought it! Apostolic purity qualifies for apostolic authority.

We have to ask ourselves, what was Paul afraid of in abusing his authority? The answer comes from Numbers 18:21–24, where God declared He had given the Levites the tithe and they had no inheritance in Israel. The penalty for abusing His authority would have been the forfeiting of His anointing that paralleled the call. Paul was very honoring of the anointing and he knew the fastest way to jeopardize it was to step over into the realm of mammon where his actions would be received as worship by satan. Paul took a stand. He would not go there! Jesus became his foremost example. He would not go where Jesus had not gone. I believe congregational intercession will result in leadership that **will not** go where Jesus has not gone, in the same spirit that Paul demonstrated. We have returned from the front lines. We have met the enemy and often they are us!

In Second Kings 5:13–16 we have a perfect example of the spirit of mammon at work as the rich man Naaman comes to Elisha for healing. Verses 13 through 16 say:

> "And his servants came near and spoke to him, and said, 'My father, if the prophet had told you to do something great, would you not have done it? How much more then, when he says to you, "Wash, and be clean"?' So he went down and dipped seven times in the Jordan, according to the saying of the man of God; and his flesh was restored like the flesh of a little child, and he was clean. Then he returned to the man of God, he and all his aids, and came and stood before him; and he said, 'Indeed, now I know that there is no God in all the earth, except in Israel; now therefore, please take a gift from your servant.' But he said, 'As the LORD lives, before whom I stand, I will receive nothing.' And he urged him to take it, but he refused."

Obeying the Spirit in giving is often a two-edged sword which God uses to deal with both the giver's and the receiver's flesh. Naaman is a very important man who always pays for what he gets. The cross is applied by Elisha's refusal. What preacher can say "No" to the biggest offering of his ministry? It is a three-edged sword in that Gehazi is tried by the same event. Naaman is healed but the LORD will not allow Elisha to take the gift. The gift becomes a substantial temptation. What is the penalty if we take advantage of God's people and take from them what we want even when God says, "No"!? Perhaps that is the message that has been lost on this next generation. How many leaders have been incarcerated in that spiritual penalty box? Dare we take an offering when God says "No"?

Verses 20–23 state:

> "But Gehazi, the servant of Elisha the man of God, said, 'Look, my master has spared Naaman this Syrian, while not receiving from his hands what he brought; but as the LORD lives, I will run after him and take something from him.' So Gehazi pursued Naaman. When Naaman saw him running after him, he got down from the chariot to meet him, and said, 'Is all well?' And he said, 'All is well. My master has sent me, saying, "Indeed, just now two young men of the sons of the prophets have come to me from the mountains of Ephraim. Please give them a talent of silver and two changes of garments."'"

If we are making twelve U. S. dollars an hour, a talent of silver in Elisha's day is the equivalent of a $2,304,000 offering. Not a bad day's work. That should pay the rent, the car payment, and anything else we might want. A slick two million! I wonder what it would cost to take that, when God said, "Don't take it"!

Verse 23 says:

> "So Naaman said, 'Please take two talents.' And he urged him, and bound two talents of silver in two bags, with two changes of garments, and handed them to two of his servants; and they carried them on ahead of him."

That is $4,608,000, plus threads! But what happened to Gazhazi? What was the penalty? Verses 26 and 27 record it:

> "Then he said to him, 'Did not my heart go with you when the man turned back from his chariot to meet you? Is it time to receive money and to receive clothing, olive groves and vineyards, sheep and oxen, male and female servants? Therefore the leprosy of Naaman shall cling to you and your descendants forever.' And he went out from his presence leprous, as white as snow."

Who received the worship of Gazhazi's actions? Why is God's response so quick and sure? The answer lies in who gains worship from our actions. Are we forfeiting the full measure of God's anointing through deception? The choices we make affect our children. How much leprosy is dispensed in the meetings we attend because true discipleship is not honored? Where is the full measure of God's authority for the end times? Why is it not more manifest? What hinders it? We must deal with mammon. We're going to have to honor the leadership of the Holy Spirit and only receive the offerings at His direction. There is no way we can teach the church to walk in the Spirit in this dimension and not do it ourselves.

In Second Corinthians 11:7–13 Paul gives us the essence of why he operated the way he did financially. He said:

> "Did I commit sin in abasing myself that you might be exalted, because I preached the gospel of God to you free of charge? I robbed other churches, taking wages from them to minister to you. And when I was present with you, and in need, I was a burden to no one, for what was lacking to me the brethren who came from Macedonia supplied. And in everything I kept myself from being burdensome to you, and so I will keep myself. As the

> truth of Christ is in me, no one shall stop me from this boasting in the regions of Achaia. Why? Because I do not love you? God knows! But what I do, I will also continue to do, that I may cut off the opportunity from those who desire an opportunity to be regarded just as we are in the things of which they boast. For such are false apostles, deceitful workers, transforming themselves into apostles of Christ."

What is the difference between the counterfeit and the true? The true don't have to take offerings. The true don't have to manipulate. They don't have to "con" their brothers. They don't even have to sell. They have the authority to do it. The true have all the same authority but they don't have to use it. Good men become counterfeits by choosing the path of manipulation, which ultimately carries them into the place of not only becoming leprous, but dispensing it upon all who participate with them at their altars! (For principles which produce impure Altars, see *Purifying the Altar* obtainable at wordatwork.org)

Paul was led to walk a different path and that is why Second Corinthians 12:14 says:

> "Now for the third time I am ready to come to you. And I will not be burdensome to you; for I do not seek yours, but you. For the children ought not to lay up for the parents, but the parents for the children."

Any apostolic network that charges the children for the maintenance of the father is laid on a foundation that is exactly opposite of what Paul did. Shouldn't we expect God to blow judgment on networks that are founded on mammon? Why don't we see the resources among the true to *give to the children*? Perhaps that will grow to be a dividing line. Paul was committed to making **disciples.** He obviously would not allow new believers to remain converts. How many can currently step up to the level of discipleship that Paul exhibited? According to the book of Philippians, very few attained this standard in Paul's day. Toward the end of his ministry he said, "I only have one person who I can totally trust, who does not **seek his own** to send to you and that is Timothy." Are we embracing the level of discipleship that Paul established?

A few years ago, I was invited to minister at what was at that time one of the largest emerging apostolic networks in America. I was excited about doing a national cutting-edge conference until I began to sense what God would have me say. The choice was reduced to either blessing the perceived visionary restoration and impartation of the "new order" or disobeying God. On the other hand, if I obeyed God I would probably be blackballed on the national stage. Sensing God's direction, I confronted the issue of manipulation, mammon, selling the gospel, and individually selling our gifts. I made the observation that the underlying principle which brought Ananias and Sapphira to destruction was routinely being practiced by each office of the five-fold ministry today. What the New Testament clearly prohibited was being universally accepted.

Apostles sold their covering by recruiting churches at five or ten percent a month. Prophets sold their words by doing conferences where (1) everyone was guaranteed a word, (2) wrist bands were sold at conferences granting exclusive access to the speakers for prophetic ministry, (3) lines for prophetic ministry were determined by differing dollar amounts, and (4) articles of clothing or jewelry were being sold promising the ministers' anointing to the highest bidder ($50,000 for a watch). Teachers were packaging, promoting, and profiting from revelation. Evangelists were printing $50 and $100 envelopes then claiming a word of knowledge, "The Lord said, twenty-five people are giving $50 and twenty are giving $100." Pastors routinely sold their seats at conferences.

What would Jesus, Peter, and Paul have said about such practices? How would they have responded? Jesus only had one issue that caused the Twelve to comment on His "lack of stability." When the Son of man encountered ministry merchandising to His people, "the meek and mild turn-the-other-cheek" Savior became a "whip the hell out of 'em" cyclone of spiritual housecleaning. When Simon the sorcerer pleaded with Peter in Acts 8, offering money for purchasing Holy Spirit power, the response seems to have emanated from the same source as Jesus' zeal. Acts 8:20–22 in the Weymouth translation says:

> "'Perish [In the NT *apo-leia* refers to the "state of perdition after death, exclusion from salvation." [3]] your money and yourself' replied Peter, 'because you have imagined that you can obtain God's free gift with money! No part or lot have you in this matter, for your heart is not right in God's sight. Repent, therefore, of this wickedness of yours, and pray to the Lord, in the hope that the purpose which is in your heart may ***perhaps*** be forgiven you."

Peter sounded like he was ready to announce another Ananias! In his mind, Simon qualified for an immediate toasting.

Paul made his stance clear in Second Corinthians 2:14–17:

> "Now thanks be to God who always leads us in triumph in Christ, and through us diffuses the fragrance of His knowledge in every place. For we are to God the fragrance of Christ among those who are being saved and among those who are perishing. To the one

> we are the aroma of death to death, and to the other the aroma of life to life. And who is sufficient for these things? For we are not, as so many, **peddling** the word of God; but as of sincerity, but as from God, we speak in the sight of God in Christ."

The Greek word translated "peddling" is *kap-ayl-yon-tase* which means to adulterate or corrupt by selling for gain. In Second Corinthians 11:7–13 Paul drew this line so the church could see the difference between the true and the counterfeit. In Second Corinthians 12:14–18 everyone Paul trained had this foundation stone.

After ministering this message at the apostolic conference, the word was rejected and personal stigmatization followed. It was reported that the night after I left they brought out preprinted $50 and $100 envelopes milking the congregation like automatic machines suck the cows dry on dairy farms. Six months later, this network was disbanded over the issue of how money was used. Hearing and responding to God's prophetic word determines the quality of our future. Is God waiting for us to move toward His example? Are we moving toward Paul's example or the world's? God is waiting on us.

Those who display purity
Sparkling with integrity
In money issues don't abuse
And in this realm none can accuse!

Jayne Houghton

Chapter 12

Executing Judgment on the Spirit of Mammon

The Great Commission in Matthew 28:18–20 says:

> "'All authority has been given to Me in heaven and on earth. Go therefore and make disciples of all the nations, baptizing them in the name of the Father and of the Son and of the Holy Spirit, teaching them to observe all things that I have commanded you; and lo, I am with you always, even to the end of the age.' Amen"

The first line of the Great Commission, where Jesus says, "All authority has been given unto Me in heaven and on earth" needs to be viewed in the context of the spiritual battle which He fought to birth and obtain that authority. Luke chapter 4 is perhaps one of the best passages revealing the origin of that warfare. Luke 4:5–6 encapsulates the battle. This passage says:

> "Then the devil, taking Him up on a high mountain, showed Him all the kingdoms of the world in a moment of time. And

> the devil said to Him, 'All this authority I will give You, and their glory; for this has been delivered to me, and I give it to whomever I wish.'"

Satan offered Jesus a shortcut in possessing the authority He was assigned to take through the cross. This authority over all the kingdoms of the world includes wealth and power. The essence of the battle involves, according to Luke 4:7, the issue of who we worship. Satan said to Jesus in verse 7, "Therefore, if You will **worship** before me, all will be Yours." Jesus refused to worship the enemy. He chose rather to pay the price of the cross and worship God! The warfare to birth and transfer that authority demands a qualifying price which must be imparted to the next generation. We not only have to understand the issues involved, but we have to disciple a generation in the principles that will qualify them to execute the judgment Jesus won that was declared by the prophets.

Psalm 149 gives us a view, from an Old Testament perspective, of what Jesus was saying in the Great Commission after He had won this victory and was imparting that authority to His people. Psalm 149:7–9, after speaking of all the different ways we praise God, defines the purpose of that praise and worship:

> ". . . To execute vengeance on the nations, And punishments on the peoples; To bind their kings with chains, And their nobles with fetters of iron; To execute on them the written judgment—This honor have all His saints."

The Great Commission imparts the divine authority that Jesus bought and paid for in His warfare with satan. It is now incumbent upon us to explore all the different principles that are involved in rising to possess that level of authority and using it effectively to fulfill prophecy. Psalm 2 has to be fulfilled, "Ask of Me, and I will give you the nations. . . ." We have to keep that God-given authority by walking the same way Jesus did to honor the authority He bought and paid for, and to use it to fulfill prophetic promises and train a generation that will wind up the age. Jesus laid down His life for us and we have to be willing to do it for each other and the next generation.

One of the very first principles the disciples had to learn was the principle of the grain of wheat, "unless . . . it falls into the ground and dies it abides alone; but if it dies, it produces much fruit." Jesus was talking to them about their own personal priorities and their own personal goals. Those had to be laid down. It is interesting to compare what Peter, James, and John (who were trained directly by Jesus) emphasized with what Paul, who came later, learned by the Holy Spirit. Paul speaks to the same issue in First Corinthians 6:19–20 when he says:

> "Or do you not know that your body is the temple of the Holy Spirit who is in you, whom you have from God, and you are not your own? For you were bought at a price; therefore glorify God in your body and in your spirit, which are God's."

One of the ways we forfeit the authority Jesus bought and paid for is allowing ourselves to be drawn into compromise. The enemy attains that through deception. I may know that homosexuality is wrong and I may take a stand and declare it, but if, through deception, I vote for a candidate who proposes anything which would statutorily protect it, such as "civil unions," then I have covenanted with death through that vote. My spiritual life is in compromise. I have opened the door inviting the spirit of perversion to attack my family. I have voted to destroy the land. In such a place, my authority has been compromised, possibly through the idol of adhering to a political party rather than obeying the living God!

Joshua was ready to cross over and take Jericho. The angel of the Lord appeared to him as a warrior and Joshua said, "Are you for us or are you for them?" The answer was "neither." We have to understand that about God. God is not a Republican and He is not a Democrat. He is GOD! And when a Republican or a Democrat takes a position against God, and we vote for that person, we forfeit our authority by covenanting with death. If you find yourself in that place, repent before the sun goes down! Jesus refused to yield such worship. He refused to worship the enemy and He bought an authority for us that we now have to maintain. We are not our own. We have been bought with a price. We have to glorify God—in our body and in our spirit, which are His! We glorify God by the way we live, by the priorities we set, by the standards we embrace. We prove we are not our own by allowing the Holy Spirit who dwells within us to direct and guide us.

The degree to which we yield to the Holy Spirit is the dimension to which we attain maturity in Christ. We're only as mature as the level at which we yield in any given circumstance or situation. Jesus was fully yielded. That has to be our goal in discipling the next generation. Will we yield to the Holy Spirit? Will we support what destroys a nation? Or will we stand against it? These are tests of discipleship and divine displays of who we worship!

Luke 16:13 says:

> "No servant can serve two masters for either he will hate the one and love the other, or else he will be loyal to the one and despise the other. You cannot serve God and mammon."

What if I conduct my ministry in such a way as to allow people to serve both? If I limit the Word, for fear of offense, I can keep people coming and possibly keep my budget intact. How does that compromise affect the people who attend? It certainly does not help them grow to the point of discipleship where they can walk as Jesus did. Conscious decisions are made consistently as to what we're going to say, what we're going to present and what level of integrity we're going to establish in our ministries. Many churches in America are populated by pastors who have been encouraged to entertain, to make things lively and not to do or say anything too controversial on a Sunday morning. Then we can pull people in and do the discipling during the week.

What would Jesus say about this approach? Was He different on Sunday then He was on Wednesday? What would Paul say? Imagine Peter speaking to this issue. "In God there is no variableness neither any shadow of turning." It is unthinkable that the Lord would be different on Sunday morning than He would be Sunday evening or Wednesday evening. Our goal is to bring believers into the image and likeness of Christ. In turn, how can we diminish the preparation to keep people and ever expect to attain the biblical goal? We forfeit our authority when we worship another kingdom called "growth and success." In today's church God's goods are being wasted daily. When we present only part of what is required, we are guilty of wasting His goods. Jesus has given us all authority in heaven and earth. How is it possible that we could waste it?

Luke 16:1–6 identifies this process. It says:

> "And He also said to His disciples: 'There was a certain rich man who had a steward, and an accusation was brought to him that this man was wasting his goods. So he called him and said to

> him, 'What is this I hear about you? Give an account of your stewardship, for you can no longer be steward.' Then the steward said within himself, 'What shall I do? For my master is taking the stewardship away from me. I cannot dig; I am ashamed to beg. I have resolved what to do, that when I am put out of the stewardship, they may receive me into their houses.' So he called every one of his master's debtors to him, and said to the first, 'How much do you owe my master?' And he said, 'A hundred measures of oil.' So he said to him, 'Take your bill, and sit down quickly and write fifty.'"

The Greek word for "wasting" in verse 1 is *dia-skor-pid-zo. Dia-skor-pid-zo* means to dispense at one's own will wherever you feel like it. The steward loses his stewardship over one issue. The issue is his will versus the Father's will. He chooses to do what he wants with what he has been given. The wisdom with which he attempts to prepare for losing his stewardship is manipulation—mammon's blood brother. He calls everyone of his master's debtors and if they owe a hundred measures he renegotiates so they only owe fifty. This is a perfect picture of the way many leaders are encouraged to facilitate growth. The idea is, don't say or do anything too offensive on Sunday morning so that we can "pull people in" and then the rest of the week, the ones who really want to grow, can be taught. This approach seems like a wonderful way to lose your stewardship. It may even qualify for being ashamed of the gospel. Can we imagine Jesus backing away from anything the Spirit would have moved Him to say on a Sunday morning? All of the people lose in that situation because they never grow, and ultimately the church loses because total truth is not presented at every opportunity. Jesus didn't do anything except what He saw the Father do and didn't say anything except what He heard the Spirit say. Any limitation on what the Spirit would say, at any point, at any time in our life, is unacceptable. This method of operation actually worships at another altar and it forfeits the purchased authority Jesus died for. Is success in numbers in the natural worth the compromise?

Verses 7 through 9 say:

> "Then he said to another, 'And how much do you owe?' So he said, 'A hundred measures of wheat.' And he said to him, 'Take your bill, and write eighty.' So the master commended the unjust steward because he had dealt shrewdly. For the sons of this world are more shrewd in their generation than the sons of light. And I say to you, make friends for yourselves by unrighteous mammon, that when you fail, they may receive you into everlasting habitations."

Perhaps the most amazing thing about this message is that Jesus ". . . commends the unjust steward." Our first question is, Why did He do that? Probably because He was being facetious. The steward was already losing his job and he was proving that he was more adept and cunning in the ways of the world than believers were in embracing the ways of light. The problem is that believers are often caught in the vice. Apparently some of them actually even like it. Maybe we should ask ourselves, Do we enjoy attending a place where we're entertained and where very little is required, and where we're never really confronted about real biblical issues that demand change? Is our church comfortable? What did Jesus mean when He said in verse 9:

> ". . . make friends for yourselves by unrighteous mammon, that when you fail, they may receive you into everlasting habitations."

"Everlasting habitations" sounds like hell! Jesus is talking about eternity in the wrong place. He has already stated "you cannot serve God and mammon." So the application of "make friends for yourselves by unrighteous mammon" should be obvious. Why did those ministers preach less than God required? Their messages apparently were more popular than, let's say, the Jonathan Edwards "Sinners in the Hands of an Angry God" type. Perhaps if we preach moderate messages, we can keep and build a larger congregation. That, of course, equals a bigger budget, enabling more money to fund more projects. But what was their end? Their end was destruction. Their end was "everlasting habitations" in what sounds like an eternal barbecue with the participating leaders on the rotisserie. Jesus gave us authority and we have to make choices about how we use it. How we use authority will honor or dishonor Jesus. There is a purpose in honoring the Lord. If we honor Him, we can grow to where He will honor us, with the assignment of executing judgment on the spirit of mammon.

Acts 4:32–34 speaks of this qualifying process:

> "Now the multitude of those who believed were of one heart and one soul; neither did anyone say that any of the things he possessed was his own, but they had all things in common. And with great power the apostles gave witness to the resurrection of the Lord Jesus. And great grace was upon them all. Nor was there anyone among them who lacked; for all who were possessors of lands or houses sold them, and brought the proceeds of the things that were sold."

By choosing not to diminish what the Holy Spirit was saying, they followed God in a process of discipleship that was about to yield a manifestation of that authority that Jesus bought and paid for. It is always dangerous to quote such a passage, because people often think that perhaps we should try duplicating what the early church did. However, there are historical circumstances which are very important prophetic factors in diminishing such an interpretation. We always have to consider historical setting in interpretation. There were two major historical issues which may have formed the foundation for the Holy Spirit leading them in mass liquidation.

Jerusalem was going to be destroyed by Titus and the Roman legions. Even though that may have been significantly in the future, it could still have had impact. There was a much closer event that was about to happen called the great persecution at Jerusalem, which scattered the church everywhere. It was obviously in God's economy because they needed to take what they had learned in Jerusalem and establish churches in many other areas. They were not exactly going to all the nations. They were camping out in the glory and the power of the anointing birthed in Jerusalem. Persecution scattered them so that they were being forced to obey the Great Commission. This is one of the historical contexts we have to apply when we interpret such a passage. It is obviously not God's will that everybody sell everything they have and live in communities. It happened at this point in church history. Can you imagine what would have happened if the apostles had diminished what Jesus was leading them to say! Having been with Jesus transformed them. They stood and proclaimed what the Spirit said regardless of the consequences. As a result, we see the power birthed and resident in their lives to deal with the spirit of mammon in such a way that it established the power of God in their generation and brought the fear of the Lord to the church.

Acts 5:1–4 records this historical event:

> "But a certain man named Ananias, with Sapphira his wife, sold a possession. And he kept back part of the proceeds, his wife also being aware of it, and brought a certain part and laid it at the apostle's feet. But Peter said, 'Ananias, why has Satan filled your heart to lie to the Holy Spirit and keep back part of the price of the land for yourself? While it remained, was it not your own? And after it was sold, was it not in your own control? Why have you conceived this thing in your heart? You have not lied to men but to God.'"

We have to remember that mammon is how satan gains worship. Jesus bought and paid for judgment on that spirit. Here we see the first manifestation of judgment on the spirit of mammon. But this brings us to a question. And the question is a simple one: Where in the American church are people being discipled so we can qualify to execute this judgment in today's world? There is certainly no absence of the spirit of mammon at work in the church-world. But where is the preparation for dealing with it and re-establishing the fear of the Lord? The emerging generation needs to be warned and insulated against the failure of their fathers. Verses 6–11 record the fruit of what Jesus bought and paid for: "**great fear** came upon all the church and upon all who heard these things." It came because there was a judgment on the spirit of mammon. They cried for an anointing so strong that neither sickness nor disease could stand in the midst. God answered their prayer and released an awesome outpouring which also brought judgment on the spirit of mammon. The church of today has to grow into the place of discipleship where we can handle the power that heals everybody because it is the same anointing that will kill anyone who harbors the spirit of mammon. Yielding to the Spirit of God in the realm of finances could be great end-time health insurance. Do we say that everything we have is our own? The goal of discipleship is to come into the full measure of the stature of Jesus Christ—to have Him fully formed in us! Judging the spirit of mammon in the early church helped everybody move toward that goal.

The prophets all saw a very specific manifestation of God's judgment on the spirit of mammon. Isaiah in both 60 and 61 speaks to that issue. Isaiah 60:5 says:

> "Then you shall see and become radiant, And your heart shall swell with joy; Because the abundance of the sea shall be turned to you, the wealth of the Gentiles shall come to you."

And chapter 61:6–7 states:

> "But you shall be named the Priests of the Lord, Men shall call you the Servants of our God. You shall eat the riches of the Gentiles, And in their glory you shall boast. Instead of your shame you shall have double honor, And instead of confusion they shall rejoice in their portion. Therefore in their land they shall possess double; Everlasting joy shall be theirs."

Isaiah saw judgment on the spirit of mammon bringing a dramatic amount of provision into the church for a purpose. The purpose, of course, is an end-time harvest, because in the harvest of nations the assignment is to not just make converts, but to make disciples. Isaiah 61 also tells us that in this process the church has a goal, ". . . Therefore in their land they shall possess double. . . ." This anointing has to be possessed. We have to qualify for it. The question is, how do we qualify? The early church qualified. They didn't qualify by receiving milk-toast messages. They qualified by hearing what the Holy Spirit said at every given service. How can we possess the promises with any less?

The latter day church is promised both the "former and the latter rain" in the same season. God will double what the early church received in anointing. Where do we go for preparation? The preparation can only come where there is a commitment to speak exactly what the Holy Spirit gives at any given time, and not water it down. Discipleship is the goal but it comes to us just like it came to the early church. It comes by yielding to the Holy Spirit and committing to say whatever He says even if it costs us half of our congregation! For the people who attend church, we have to make a decision. Do we want truth? Do we want everything God has? Or do we want spiritual entertainment with fun and occasional excitement?

Does God give us a hint as to the timing of what Isaiah saw? In James 5:1–3 we are told:

> "Come now, you rich, weep and howl for your miseries that are coming upon you! Your riches are corrupted, and your garments are moth-eaten. Your gold and silver are corroded, and their corrosion will be a witness against you and will eat your flesh like fire. You have heaped up treasure in the last days."

The last days identify the season. Two things have to merge together for fulfillment. We have to find a significant number of people that are willing to embrace the cross and submit to God's preparation so we can qualify for what the prophets saw and the apostles declared. Secondly, it is impossible to execute judgment on the spirit of mammon if it has any place in us. Verse 4 documents what has to come from those in ministry:

> "Indeed the wages of the laborers who mowed your fields, which you kept back by fraud, cry out; and the cries of the reapers have reached the ears of the Lord of Sabaoth."

"The Lord of the Sabaoth" is a phrase that is used in the Old Testament for the God of war. The Greek word for "cry out" is *krad-zo. Krad-zo* is also used of Peter in Matthew 14 when he steps out of the boat to walk on the water to go to Jesus. Matthew 14:28–30 says:

> "And Peter answered Him and said, 'Lord, if it is You, command me to come to You on the water.' So He said, 'Come.' And when Peter had come down out of the boat, he walked on the water to go to Jesus. But when he saw that the wind was boisterous, he was afraid; and beginning to sink he cried out [*krad-zo*], saying, 'Lord save me!' And immediately Jesus stretched out His hand and caught him, and said to him, 'O you of little faith, why did you doubt?'"

Peter was drowning. The cry of drowning men, ministries, or circumstances when believing God for the necessary funds to disciple cities and nations, is an essential part of the equation for seeing this fulfillment. It would appear that there are an abundance of ministries who are currently occupying this position. Qualifying is a crucifixion process all its own. The Twelve had a terribly difficult time after Jesus' death. Discouragement reigned. It is hard but the Holy Spirit is recruiting.

Another part of this preparational process is identified in Romans 12:1 which says:

> "I beseech you therefore, brethren, by the mercies of God, that you present your bodies a living sacrifice, holy, acceptable to God, which is your reasonable service."

"Reasonable service" here could also just as easily be translated "reasonable worship." Growing up into the concept that **we are**

not our own is not an option. It is a way of life, as we daily present ourselves to Jesus as a living sacrifice. Walking with Him is a way of life that has to be embraced. This way of life that has to be strengthened and encouraged is only found in Scripture. How often is it taught?

In Second Kings 5:16, Elisha exemplifies what we are told to do in Romans 12:1. With a $4.6 million offering in his face it says:

> "But he said, 'As the LORD lives, before whom I stand, I will receive nothing.' And he urged him to take it, but he refused."

Walking in the spirit means saying "no" to what we wouldn't say "no" to in the natural. Saying "no" to $4.6 million gives Elisha the authority to execute judgment on the spirit of mammon. Verse 27 records the event when he says:

> "'Therefore the leprosy of Naaman shall cling to you and your descendants forever.' And he went out from his presence leprous, as white as snow."

Did Peter execute judgment on the spirit of mammon in Acts 5? Did Paul execute judgment on the spirit of mammon in Acts 13:10–11 when he said:

> ". . . 'O full of all deceit and all fraud, you son of the devil, you enemy of all righteousness, will you not cease perverting the straight ways of the Lord? And now, indeed, the hand of the Lord is upon you, and you shall be blind, not seeing the sun for a time.' And immediately a dark mist fell on him, and he went around seeking someone to lead him by the hand."

Paul had no problem executing judgment on that spirit. Where is the authority in the church to execute judgment on the spirit of mammon today? Why is it absent? Why is there no fear of the Lord in the church? We have a job to do in discipleship in preparing people, and we have been remiss in bringing them into this dimension. How many times, on a Sunday morning, are the straight ways of the Lord perverted? How many times are the straight ways of the Lord diminished by 50 percent or 20 percent or 80 percent so we can keep a congregation? Paul would have never done that. Jesus wouldn't do it. It was unthinkable to Peter. It apparently was unthinkable to James. The Lord's ways are straight. No man can think crooked and live straight! The only way to live straight is to think straight, and the only way to think straight is to consistently hear the unadulterated word of God. Our mind has to be renewed. This is the level of discipleship that has to come to the next generation.

In Luke 12:49 Jesus said after teaching on the parable of the faithful steward, "I came to send fire on the earth, and how I wish it were already kindled!"

When the fire falls, who will direct it? Who will announce it? Who will proclaim it? Developing faithfulness as a disciple qualifies us to understand, walk in, and proclaim the word of the Lord as prompted by the Holy Spirit on a daily basis, preparing us to fulfill what the prophets saw and proclaimed. Anything less is not the discipleship that God requires for our generation.

Barnabas is a perfect example. His ministry begins shortly after we first meet him in Acts 4:36–37 when he sells his productive land, the kind of land that a Levite was not allowed to have, and lays the money at the apostle's feet. His action sets the stage for judgment on the spirit of mammon as it unfolds in Acts chapter 5. The obedience of Barnabas to the prompting of the Holy Spirit seems to be contrasted with the manipulation of Ananias and Sapphira. Jesus promised the Twelve they would do the works He did and greater! Which is the greater work, raising the dead or making them dead? The answer is making them dead! Did Jesus prepare them for such a season?

Luke 12 is possibly one of the most intense chapters of discipleship recorded in the New Testament, where Jesus is preparing and promising the Twelve that they can have the full measure of anointing available and walk as He walked. In verses 1–12 Jesus warns them about hypocrisy. Paul put it this way, "You can't pervert the straight ways of the Lord." Anybody who is going to qualify for dispensing God's judgment in appointed seasons has to walk the straight ways of the Lord. So He begins chapter 12 with warnings about hypocrisy, but then immediately in verses 13–15 transitions to the primary area of disqualifying warfare and the spirit of mammon. These verses state:

> "Then one from the crowd said to Him, 'Teacher, tell my brother to divide the inheritance with me.' But He said to him, 'Man, who made Me a judge or an arbitrator over you?' And He said to them, 'Take heed and beware of covetousness,' for one's life does not consist in the abundance of the things he possesses.'"

Jesus made it clear to the Twelve that their life did not depend on a "balance sheet." Wherever we place value, our heart follows. So we have to ask ourselves, if the Lord were to look at our life, where would our abundance be? Would it be in what we possess, or what we have produced for the Kingdom, including character and who we are? Is who we are more valuable than what we possess? It certainly is to God and it needs to be to us. Do we treasure what is eternal? How much of what we're attempting to gain would fall in the category of "abundance of things he possesses?" How much of our life benefits the eternal? Are we contributing to fulfilling God's will in our generation? These questions help us assess our growth in Christ-likeness.

In verses 16–21 Jesus taught the parable of the rich man whose ground yielded plentifully, so he said to himself, "What should I do. I don't have any room to store my crops. I know, I'll tear down the old barns and I will build bigger barns." Of course immediately the Lord said, "You fool! This night your soul will be required of you. . . ."

Jesus emphasized the necessity of living in the spirit. Where is our heart? Have we placed a greater value on being successful financially, or on building the character of Christ into our existence? Jesus made it clear to them that if they were ever going to execute judgment on the spirit of mammon, they had to get their priorities straight. He didn't say He wouldn't bless them. He didn't say they couldn't be very, very successful. What He said to them was they had to get their priorities straight. Their chief priority was to lay up in heaven. In verses 22–34, Jesus continued to build on the theme that they didn't have to worry about provision, for God cared for them. He loved them and if He took care of the birds, He would take care of them. He exhorted them to seek *first* the Kingdom and all these things would be added to them. In verse 34 He said, "For where your treasure is, there your heart will be also."

The chief issue in their preparation at this stage was the positioning of the heart. If the Twelve could position their heart in the right place, they could grow to find themselves in the right place at the right time for God's very best. Eleven made it. Will we join that group? I'm sure Peter had no idea that one day he would be executing judgment on the spirit of mammon. His preparation was moving toward that goal. God's goal for the Twelve was not getting caught up building their own kingdoms, or building businesses, or securing their guaranteed provision. His goal for them demanded walking in the spirit. Walking in the spirit requires godly personal choices. They would never be able to fulfill God's will if they didn't grow in that dimension. How much time do we give to growing in the realm of the spirit? Are we preparing for what is about to break forth? The Lord spoke to me one time concerning personal choices. Integrity in private where no eye can see produces power in public where every eye can see!

Matthew 5:20–26 makes a very important point about our qualifying to execute judgment on the spirit of mammon:

> "For I say to you, that unless your righteousness exceeds the righteousness of the scribes and Pharisees, you will by no means enter the kingdom of heaven. You have heard that it was said to those of old, 'You shall not murder' and whoever murders will be in danger of the judgment. But I say to you that whoever is angry with his brother without a cause shall be in danger of the judgment. And whoever says to his brother, 'Raca' shall be in danger of the council. But whoever says, 'You fool!' shall be in danger of hell fire. Therefore if you bring your gift to the altar, and there remember that your brother has something against you, leave your gift there before the altar, and go your way. First be reconciled to your brother, and then come and offer your gift. Agree with your adversary quickly, while you are on the way with him, lest your adversary deliver you to the judge, the judge hand you over to the officer, and you are thrown into prison. Assuredly, I say to you, you will by no means get out of there till you have paid the last penny."

Jesus set a standard that we must embrace. Our growth and commitment to that standard dictates certain actions when an offense arises. The key is verse 23:

> "Therefore if you bring your gift to the altar, and there remember that your brother has something against you, leave your gift there before the altar, and go your way. First be reconciled to your brother, and then come and offer your gift."

Jesus emphasized the condition of relationships within the church family. How shall we conduct ourselves in the church? If we find that somebody has something against us, we have an obligation to go and make it right. If we don't, it hinders our financial flow. It brings us into a spiritual prison. We are told we can't get out until we've paid the last penny. This is not optional Christianity. This is discipleship that is necessary if we are going to qualify for the full measure of the anointing that is promised in Luke 12. This is not something we can think about and decide one day that it is optional. Jesus said, "Agree with your adversary quickly." Financial prison results from not acknowledging our own personal offenses and actively pursuing reconciliation. We cannot afford to be the offender. We usually can't afford to take an offense either. Money and agreement is a very powerful force throughout Scripture. God honors humility and reconciliation. Humility is exercised when we go to somebody we have offended and make it right. God loves the humble and He draws very close to them. This is a part of our discipleship that we cannot ignore.

In Luke 12:35–37, Jesus offers a major promise to all who incorporate this level of discipleship into their lives. When He comes He will find them, He will gird Himself, make them sit, and He will come and serve them. Can you imagine being served by the

Creator of the Universe? Yet, Jesus promised it so we know it is going to happen.

We know we will be battling the thief at many junctures. It says in verses 38–40, for those who are not actively pursuing Christ-likeness, that He will be a thief to them and when God becomes a thief no one can stop our losses! That is something we definitely want to avoid and the only way to do it is active discipleship.

In verses 41–42 we find the Lord has a very specific goal for our discipleship. It is that we make a full contribution as He has ordained within our gifting and calling. We must qualify and birth the necessary anointing to accomplish what God has assigned. We must possess the full measure without any hesitation. It must be released to accomplish God's ultimate call. There is a point when what has been promised comes into manifestation. When it is resident, we don't have to ask for it anymore. We don't have to pray for it anymore. It has been birthed. We have it. And we can dispense it at any time. Acts 3 records this season for Peter when he says, "Silver and gold I do not have, but what **I do have** I give you: In the name of Jesus Christ of Nazareth, rise up and walk."

It's birthed. It's resident. And it is operational. It can be dispensed to anyone.

In Luke 12:43–44 we are told, "Blessed is that servant whom his master will find so doing when he comes. Truly, I say to you that he will make him ruler over all that he has."

The issue of being "ruler" over all His goods is attaining the full measure of anointing that parallels our gifting and calling. We should ask ourselves, What happens to the gifting and calling of the one-talent individual who hid his money in the sand and didn't do anything with it? He didn't develop it. He didn't move on into discipleship. He didn't make anything for the Master. It was taken from him and given to the one who had ten.

What happens when Jesus says, "From this point on I make you ruler over all My goods"? He is saying, "I withhold nothing within the borders and boundaries of your gifting and calling." The power came in the early church after they withheld nothing from the Lord and each other in Acts 2:44–46. God still reciprocates in kind today. Acts 3:6 demonstrates a resident anointing where nothing is withheld from them, "Silver and gold I do not have, but what **I do have** I give you: In the name of Jesus Christ of Nazareth, rise up and walk."

They possessed the double anointing. They had been obedient to the Holy Spirit. They demonstrated the discipleship they learned from Jesus and followed in His footsteps and consequently He made them ruler over all His goods. Acts 5:15–16 describe the same season:

> ". . . so that they brought the sick out into the streets and laid them on beds and couches, that at least the shadow of Peter passing by might fall on some of them. Also a multitude gathered from the surrounding cities to Jerusalem, bringing sick people and those who were tormented by unclean spirits, and they were **all healed**."

Did the early church become "ruler over **all** His goods"? They certainly did in the realm of deliverance and healing. They gained a reputation. It was well earned. The preparation which preceded the manifestation of healing was confronting the spirit of mammon.

They had seasons where everybody was healed, but it began when they paid the price in discipleship and qualified to execute judgment on the spirit of mammon. One of the problems with the church today is that we want the blessing but we don't want to qualify to execute the judgment. Are we perverting the straight ways of the Lord? The pattern has been set. How can we change it? We have to make some choices in following the straight ways of the Lord. How we are going to operate financially determines victory or defeat in the battle against mammon. The choice is ours. Perhaps God is waiting on us.

Are we after growth and success
Spreading enjoyment and happiness
Do we prefer what doesn't offend
Perhaps the heart of God we rend

Jayne Houghton

Chapter 13

Restoring the Fear of the Lord

Paul set the gold standard for discipleship in Second Corinthians 5:9–11 when he said:

> "Therefore we make it our aim, whether present or absent, to be well pleasing to Him. For we must all appear before the judgment seat of Christ, that each one may receive the things done in the body, according to what he has done, whether good or bad. **Knowing, therefore, the terror of the Lord**, we persuade men; but we are well-known to God, and I also trust are well-known in your consciences."

The word "terror" comes from the Greek word *pho-bos. Pho-bos* generally means godly fear or a reverential sense of accountability. It also means to put one in fear or to experience a sudden sense of divine accountability. Paul says this anointing was part of his life. It was present or imparted when he ministered. That leaves us with a nagging question. Where is it when we minister? Where is it when our friends minister? What happens when our pastors minister? Do our prophets impart this? Do our teachers have it? Do we have to have an apostolic call to qualify? Is being knocked off a donkey, or parallel experience, necessary for this impartation? This was obviously the foundational underpinning for everything Paul did and said. He used *pho-bos* to persuade like a mechanic uses tools to tune an engine. Where is it in the church today? Paul acted like this was commonplace, that every ministry should impart this. If Paul was right, something might have been lost generationally and the question is, where do we go to find it?

Is there a reverential sense of awe and accountability imparted in the church where we attend? Does this ever fall in our services? Or do we have Holy Spirit feel-good meetings where we are satisfied to meet God halfway in worship, having a few "My children" prophetic words followed by a good message, praying for the sick and repeat, repeat, repeat Sunday after Sunday! The **fear of the Lord** could change a heart forever, once encountered! Are we missing, in the American church, the real depth of what the early church experienced? If we are, how do we recover it? The answer to recovering it may be in identifying all the ways it was imparted and pursuing those as led by the Holy Spirit. Either Paul caught it or it caught him. Whether it came by seeking access to the third heaven or being knocked off his donkey, it is worth pursuing. Most of us will not ask to be knocked flat and being caught up is nothing to seek unless we first learn to shut up about spiritual experiences that belong in the closet of personal privacy, because they can so easily mislead the church.

Matthew 14:22–24 describes one potential avenue:

> "Immediately Jesus made His disciples get into the boat and go before Him to the other side, while He sent the multitudes away. And when He had sent the multitudes away, He went up on a

mountain by Himself to pray. And when evening had come, He was alone there. But the boat was now in the middle of the sea, tossed by the waves, for the wind was contrary."

Jesus had been up on the mountain in prayer. The disciples were going to the other side of the lake in a boat. Jesus appeared to them walking on the water. They thought it was a ghost and verse 26 tells us ". . . they cried out for fear." The Greek word translated "fear" is our root word *pho-bos*. We can conclude that Jesus imparts fear in how we encounter Him. Did the disciples catch the fear of the Lord during their training? Should receiving the fear of the Lord be one of the major marks that distinguishes converts from disciples? One element of the transition from convert status to **disciple** status is catching the fear of the Lord!

Matthew 28:1–4 reveals another way fear can come:

"Now after the Sabbath, as the first day of the week began to dawn, Mary Magdalene and the other Mary came to see the tomb. And behold, there was a great earthquake; for an angel of the Lord descended from heaven, and came and rolled back the stone from the door, and sat on it. His countenance was like lightening, and his clothing as white as snow. And the guards shook for fear (*pho-bos*) of him, and became like dead men."

In verse 4 we find the same Greek word *pho-bos* translated "fear" but here the guards are shaking instead of crying out and suddenly they become motionless. They are paralyzed with the measure of fear that is imparted when they see the angel. Angels can impart the **fear of the Lord.** One angelic encounter could change us forever!

In Mark 4:36–41, we see a third way the **fear of the Lord** can come:

> "Now when they had left the multitude, they took Him along in the boat as He was. And other little boats were also with Him. And a great windstorm arose, and the waves beat into the boat, so that it was already filling. But He was in the stern, asleep on a pillow. And they awoke Him and said to Him. 'Teacher, do You not care that we are perishing?' Then He arose and rebuked the wind, and said to the sea, 'Peace, be still!' And the wind ceased and there was a great calm. But He said to them, 'Why are you so fearful? How is it that you have no faith?' And they **feared exceedingly**, and said to one another, 'Who can this be, that even the wind and the sea obey Him!'"

When Jesus exercised faith against the raging ocean, and God honored it, in verse 41, "they feared exceedingly, and said to one another, 'Who can this be, that even the wind and the sea obey Him!'"

Faith proclamations that God honors can impart the fear of the Lord. Surely we can raise up a generation that will feel comfortable speaking to the weather. Surely we can speak to the adversity of nature and God will honor it. Manifestations of divine authority in our midst can impart the fear of the Lord. It can come when God miraculously answers prayer or answers a faith command. Faith commands should not be unfamiliar to us because James prescribes them for anyone who is sick. Let him call for the elders of the church, they will pray the prayer of faith, the prayer of faith will save the sick and the Lord will raise him up. Surely the faith command is something that every one of us should learn because it is part of our covenantal heritage. "Peace be still" can be spoken to any storm and should be routinely. Every generation needs elementary faith teaching. Faith teaching without the cross being applied to one's life builds arrogance and presumption, usually ending in devastating disappointment. Faith teaching with the cross is freeing and quite fulfilling eventually.

Luke 1:11–12 records another manifestation of the **fear of the Lord:**

> "Then an angel of the Lord appeared to him, standing on the right side of the altar of incense. And when Zacharias saw him, he was troubled, and **fear fell upon him**."

The fear of the Lord can come as a cloud and just settle on people depending on their circumstances and what is happening in a visitation. It is nice to know that fear can come many different ways. Divine encounters are to be sought. Usually in Scripture when they come, people change. They often walk with a whole different perspective from that point on. Angelic visitations usually accompany seasonal and generational changes. When God's generals go home to be with Him, the seasons change. An identifiable transitional period has occurred every forty years since the restoration of Holy Spirit power, marked by Azusa Street. The transition between leadership generations may last ten years, but it exists. The fear of the Lord cannot flow through us to others unless it first comes to us. The reason Paul could impart it is because he had received it. Had he never received it, he would not have been able to impart it. Perhaps we need to seek the fear of the Lord. Mixed seed ministries emerge when there is no fear of the Lord.

Luke 1 verses 57 through 65 teach that the fear of the Lord comes through prophetic fulfillment:

> "Now Elizabeth's full time came for her to be delivered, and she brought forth a son. When her neighbors and relatives heard how

> the Lord had shown great mercy on her, they rejoiced with her. Now so it was, on the eighth day, that they came to circumcise the child; and they would have called him by the name of his father, Zacharias, And his mother answered and said, 'No; he shall be called John.' But they said to her, 'There is no one among your relatives who is called by this name.' So they made signs to his father—what he would have him called. And he asked for a writing tablet, and wrote, saying, 'His name is John.' And they all marveled. Immediately his mouth was opened and his tongue loosed, and he spoke, praising God. Then **fear** came on all who dwelt around them; and all these sayings were discussed throughout all the hill country of Judea."

When John the Baptist was born they were naming him an unusual name for their family. They asked Zacharias and he had to write the name. Once he penned "John," he was healed, his mouth was opened, his tongue loosed and he started to speak. His first words were "His name is John." This prophetic fulfillment, when it was discussed throughout the region of Judea, released the **fear of the Lord.** Fulfillment of prophecy can release God's fear.

In Luke 5:20–26 when men brought a paralyzed friend to Jesus and couldn't get him inside because of the crowd, they took the roof apart and lowered him before Jesus. Verses 20–26 state:

> "So when He saw their faith, He said to him, 'Man, your sins are forgiven you.' And the scribes and the Pharisees began to reason, saying, 'Who is this who speaks blasphemies? Who can forgive sins but God alone?' But when Jesus perceived their thoughts, He answered and said to them, 'Why are you reasoning in your hearts? Which is easier, to say, "Your sins are forgive you," or to say, "Rise up and walk"? But that you may know that the Son of

> Man has power on earth to forgive sins'—He said to the man who was paralyzed, 'I say to you, arise, take up your bed, and go to your house.' Immediately he rose up before them, took up what he had been lying on, and departed to his own house, glorifying God. And they were all amazed, and they glorified God and were filled with **fear**, saying, 'We have seen strange things today!'"

If we are to do the works Jesus did, we should expect the same results. Dramatic healing can be another avenue that releases the *pho-bos* of God. The fear of the Lord seems to be available to all who want it.

Luke 7:11–16 describes another miraculous event that imparts the **fear of the Lord.** Jesus encountered a funeral procession in a city called Nain, where a widow had lost her son. Jesus had compassion on her and said, "Do not weep." Verses 14–16 record:

> "Then He came and touched the open coffin, and those who carried him stood still. And He said, 'Young man, I say to you, arise.' And he who was dead sat up and began to speak. And He presented him to his mother. Then **fear** came upon all, and they glorified God, saying, 'A great prophet has risen up among us'; and, 'God has visited His people.'"

Raising the dead can release the fear of God in a city, or certainly in everybody who sees the event or meets the young man who was raised.

In Luke 21:25–28 Jesus had been asked what would be the sign of His Second Coming. He said:

> "And there will be signs in the sun, in the moon, and in the stars; and on the earth distress of nations, with perplexity, the sea and

> the waves roaring; men's hearts failing them from **fear and the expectation of those things which are coming on the earth**, for the powers of heaven will be shaken. Then they will see the Son of Man coming in a cloud with power and great glory. Now when these things begin to happen, look up and lift up your heads, because your redemption draws near."

As we move into the latter days, a dramatic increase of geologic disruption in the heavens, in the oceans, and in the earth have been prophesied. Until recently no one expected a devastating tsunami. Mountains will blow and lava will flow. These events are going to cause men's hearts to fail from fear. The same events bringing fear to the unbeliever should bring biblical confirmation to the Saints. Jesus tells the church when we see these things happening to begin to rejoice. We should be among the group that dispenses the fear of the Lord or can certainly interpret it to people in such a season. Jesus said the nations would be distressed. He said nation would rise against nation. We are certainly seeing that with the increase of terrorism. How can there be any change as long as man continues to rebel against God? A dramatic increase in fear-causing events is coming. We have an obligation to prepare the church to speak to the world as dramatic devastations increase. The world is incapable of seeing God's hand in all that is going to unfold, whereas the church can be prepared to reap a harvest if we can persuade men.

Any nation which approves homosexual/lesbian marriage has no **fear of the Lord** in its leaders. How can a nation's leaders have godly fear if there is none in the church? What happens to our country may be laid at the feet of the church. We have to birth what God has made available to us. Birthing it means seeking it. Preparing for and understanding it precedes receiving it, which precedes imparting it.

John 7:10–13 records another kind of fear that has to be overcome which many often face:

> "But when His brothers had gone up, then He also went up to the feast, not openly, but as it were in secret. Then the Jews sought Him at the feast, and said, 'Where is He?' And there was much murmuring among the people concerning Him. Some said, 'He is good': others said, 'No, on the contrary, He deceives the people.' However, no one spoke openly of Him for **fear of the Jews**."

The Bible records three realms of fear: (1) fear generated by government, (2) the fear of religious authorities and what they'll do, and finally (3) we have the fear of the Lord. What happens if these groups come into conflict? Which fear wins if government says **stop** worshiping Jesus? We have to prepare a generation to dispense the **fear of the Lord.** The next generation can be free from the fear of government and religious systems. Natural catastrophes like earthquakes and floods are coming. We might as well prepare for that. We have to trust God to carry us through. The question is, will we be free from the fear of Secular Humanism, America's godless new religion? Will we be free from the fear of man and the fear of what the government can do? If we're not, we will not be ready to walk through the last days. Discipleship has a goal. The goal is that the fear of the Lord is paramount and helps us overcome when any other fear emerges.

In John 19:38 we are told:

> "After this, Joseph of Arimathea, being a disciple of Jesus, but secretly, for **fear of the Jews**, asked Pilate that he might take away the body of Jesus. . . ."

Jesus couldn't even be buried apart from the fear of the Jews. The early disciples had to battle different realms of fear. I'm sure there are many believers who have the fear of government, the fear of police, fear of the FBI, fear of Muslims, fear of Islamic terrorists—fear of the unknown. What will overcome this great variety of groups to be feared? There is only one answer—the **fear of the Lord.** Where are we in that progression? The condition of our nation would indicate we are far from godly fear in the church.

What do we expect Jesus to do when competing fears arise? John 20:19 declares:

> "Then, the same day at evening, being the first day of the week, when the doors were shut where the disciples were assembled, **for fear of the Jews**, Jesus came and stood in the midst, and said to them, 'Peace be with you.'"

We can expect Jesus to come in the midst of us and impart His peace. God has to give us peace when the fear of others captures our minds. How many live their life in captivity, with fear of one group or another dominating them? God is calling us to the **fear of the Lord.** Jesus was very clear about **who** we should fear, and it is not government entities like the police and FBI who are called God's ministers for our good and should be supported. We should not fear Islamic terrorists. We should not fear the IRS. What happens when the fear of one group or another, instead of the fear of God, dictates behavior? When fear of any other thing, group, entity, person, or event is above the fear of God, we have a paralyzing conflict! The **fear of the Lord** must be restored to the church. How will it come? Only God can choose the avenue. Fortunately He has a large variety of venues from which to choose. We have not, because we ask not, according to James. We should ask according to our gifting and calling. *Asking* is our part—restoring is God's part! Experiencing God intimately creates awesome respect. Seeing the reward of evil doers creates fear.

Acts 2:41–43 records:

> "Then those who gladly received his word were baptized; and that day about three thousand souls were added to them. And they continued steadfastly in the apostles' doctrine and fellowship, in the breaking of bread, and in prayers. **Then fear came upon every soul**, and many wonders and signs were done through the apostles."

This is my favorite avenue. In the early church, the **fear of the Lord** came as a gift. It was free. It just manifested one day on everybody, possibly as the signs, wonders, and miracles were done, but possibly it just corporately fell like a cloud. Isn't it nice to know that it's possible for the fear of the Lord to come as a free gift, that God may just do it one day when we're gathered together? Wouldn't that be a blessing? If we've never asked for the fear of the Lord perhaps this is a good time to ask, and we can ask for it to come like the gifts of the Spirit, to just manifest in our midst. God did it for the early church and He can do it for us!

In my early years of ministry, I thought the only way the fear of the Lord could ever be restored to the church was if we could duplicate Acts 5. Acts 5:1–5 states:

> "But a certain man named Ananias, with Sapphira his wife, sold a possession. And he kept back part of the proceeds, his wife also being aware of it, and brought a certain part and laid it at the

> apostles' feet. But Peter said, 'Ananias, why has Satan filled your heart to lie to the Holy Spirit and keep back part of the price of the land for yourself? While it remained, was it not your own? And after it was sold, was it not in your own control? Why have you conceived this thing in your heart? You have not lied to men but to God.' Then Ananias, hearing these words, fell down and breathed his last. So **great fear** came upon all those who heard these things."

Perhaps this is the last thing we should seek; however, it was very effective. Not just the fear of the Lord came on all those who even heard about it, but "great fear" came on them. In today's church, with watered-down messages to attract and keep people, who would be more qualified for an Ananias and Saphira event, those who occupy pulpits or pews? Considering the principle "to whom much is given much is required," we would have to conclude those in the pulpit much more likely targets. I trust and I hope that God will choose all the other avenues that Scripture offers in bringing the **fear of the Lord.** Perhaps the avenue will depend on our intercession. It happened in the early church and it will undoubtedly happen in the days ahead. Let's hope we can attain it as a gift. When is the last time you felt a deep reverential sense of accountability imparted to you when you heard a message? God is going to restore this authority. Let's trust we can bring it to the church like Paul did. Having experienced it himself, it became a part of his life, and whenever he opened his mouth the words carried the weight of meeting the God who dislodged him from a donkey, blinded him, and turned him from adversary to agent. Fear can't flow through us till it first comes to us.

Acts 9:28–31 says:

> "So he was with them at Jerusalem, coming in and going out. And he spoke boldly in the name of the Lord Jesus and disputed against the Hellenists, but they attempted to kill him. When the brethren found out, they brought him down to Caesarea and sent him out to Tarsus. Then the churches throughout all Judea, Galilee, and Samaria had peace and were edified. And walking in the **fear of the Lord** and in the comfort of the Holy Spirit, they were multiplied."

Isn't it interesting that Paul's testimony included an attempted assassination—but they couldn't kill him. And Paul, apparently, brought an impartation of the fear of the Lord. They walked it simultaneously with the "comfort of the Holy Spirit." "The fear of the Lord and the comfort of the Holy Spirit" are not mutually exclusive. They can go together. Perhaps we could even argue they should go together. "The fear of the Lord and comfort of the Holy Spirit" provide godly stability. With the **fear of the Lord** we persuade men. It's coming. We have to birth it in order to impart it to the next generation.

Acts 19:11–17 discusses the unusual miracles done by the hands of Paul. It also portrays the seven sons of Sceva, who tried to act on Paul's revelation. They were attempting to do deliverance based on the relationship that Paul had with the Lord. It didn't work very well. Verses 15–17 state:

> "And the evil spirit answered and said, 'Jesus I know, and Paul I know; but who are you?' Then the man in whom the evil spirit was leaped on them, overpowered them, and prevailed against them, so that they fled out of that house naked and wounded. This became known both to all Jews and Greeks dwelling in

> Ephesus; **and fear fell on them all**, and the name of the Lord Jesus was magnified."

What is interesting about this passage is ". . . Jews and Greeks heard this story dwelling in Ephesus, and fear fell on them all." God is not limited to bringing the fear of the Lord through those of us who seek Him for it. He can bring it through religious people that don't have any understanding or knowledge of Him, who are just trying to do something they have seen a believer do. They were trying to mimic something they had seen. What a harvest field Ephesus must have been at this stage. If the church attains the full measure of anointing available, we may see a repeat of unusual events like this with the restoration of the fear of the Lord as a result.

Romans 3:9–18 discusses the spiritual condition of the world, consistently exemplified by some in high position. Verse 18 says, "There is no fear of God before their eyes." Who will God hold responsible when there is no fear of God before their eyes? The answer is obvious. We the church are responsible and it is up to us to do something about it. The difference between the unbeliever and believer becomes obvious when we see the righteousness of God revealed in life through faith in Jesus Christ. Jesus is Truth. Truth sets a person free. But that freedom demands the fear of God in order to persuade men. If we have the freedom and not the fear of God, there is very little persuasion for the church to impart.

Without the fear of God, the church loses its persuasion with the government and courts. Has the church lost its ability to persuade? It would appear we have. We've certainly faded in persuading the Supreme Court. Is God going to restore the **fear of the Lord** with which we persuade men? He is, if we'll seek Him for it. He may do it without seeking Him for it, but we're in such a dangerous place with the condition of our nation, how can the church go one more month without seeking to restore the fear of the Lord? Converts don't seem to be concerned about the fear of the Lord. The future of the country hangs in the balance. Disciples have no choice but to birth it!

Romans 13:1–4 says:

> "Let every soul be subject to the governing authorities. For there is no authority except from God, and the authorities that exist are appointed by God. Therefore whoever resists the authority resists the ordinance of God, and those who resist will bring judgment on themselves. For rulers are not a terror to good works, but to evil. Do you want to be unafraid of the authority? Do what is good, and you will have praise from the same. For he is God's minister to you for good. But if you do evil, be afraid; for he does not bear the sword in vain; for he is God's minister, an avenger to execute wrath on him who practices evil."

In God's economy, rulers, leaders, senators, representatives, and Supreme Court justices are supposed to be "not a terror to good works but evil." Government is God's minister for good and it can only be God's minister for good if it is a terror and brings fear on those who do evil. Then and only then does government become God's minister. Government, according to this passage, is supposed to execute God's wrath on those who practice evil. Without the **fear of the Lord,** what God intended is reversed. How is it that we now have perverse and filthy representatives in government who are sanctioning and blessing evil, like homosexual marriage or its equal, "civil unions"? Where is the **fear of God** in the government? It doesn't exist. It's not there and it can't be if it is not first in the church. How can the church pass the fear of God on to the government if the church doesn't have it? Government, when it works right, brings fear to evil doers. And when it is not working right, it fills a land with iniquity, guaranteeing judgment. How far down the road are we in that progression of events? The answer is in the magnitude of future terrorist events. Will God hold the church accountable for the condition of the government? It may be that He already has.

First Timothy 2:1–4 says:

"Therefore I exhort first of all that supplications, prayers, intercessions, and giving of thanks be made for all men, for kings and all who are in authority, that we may lead a quiet and peaceable life in all godliness and reverence. For this is good and acceptable in the sight of God our Savior, who desires all men to be saved and to come to the knowledge of the truth."

When we read passages like this there is no doubt that we are accountable. Since He calls us to pray for government, it is incumbent on us to bring the fear of the Lord to them. We can't bring it if we don't have it. Where is the **fear of the Lord** in the American church? Is the failure to impact government because we have settled for converts and not gone on to make disciples? The repercussions of not making disciples are continuing at a dramatic pace for both the church and the nation!

Paul established an exemplary model mentioned in First Corinthians 2:1–5:

"And I, brethren, when I came to you, did not come with excellence of speech or of wisdom declaring to you the testimony of God. For I determined not to know anything among you except Jesus Christ and Him crucified. I was with you in weakness, **in**

> **fear**, and in much trembling, And my speech and my preaching were not with persuasive words of human wisdom, but in demonstration of the Spirit and of power, that your faith should not be in the wisdom of men but in the power of God."

When Paul went somewhere to preach, one of the things he imparted was the **fear of the Lord** and that impartation of the fear of the Lord came through the power of God. This is the model that Scripture outlines for us. Jesus bought the fear of the Lord for us with His sacrifice. We have sought the power of God for healing and for deliverance but we haven't sought it specifically to impart the fear of the Lord. It may be at this juncture that there is no greater gift we could leave to our succeeding generation than the birthing of the **fear of the Lord.** The future of our nation hangs in the balance.

Second Corinthians 5:9–11 says:

> "Therefore we make it our aim, whether present or absent, to be well pleasing to Him. For we must all appear before the judgment seat of Christ, that each one may receive the things done in the body, according to what he has done, whether good or bad. Knowing, therefore, the terror of the Lord, we persuade men; but we are well-known to God, and I also trust are well-known in your consciences."

Paul lets us see the transparency of his heart. It was unthinkable to operate any other way. Paul would have marveled that anyone could step into the pulpit and not impart the fear of the Lord. It would have been unconscionable and nearly out of the realm of possibility. He would have said we were totally incapable of persuading men if we had not experienced the **fear of the Lord.** It is what gives credibility to our words. It is the spiritual impartation that changes people's lives. When we read his words, we have to ask ourselves, where is this anointing in the church today? Why can't we impart it to the government? How can we restore it? James said, "We have not because we ask not." Converts may not see the need but disciples should! The question is, Are the disciples asking? Are we afraid to ask? Are we willing to abandon ourselves to such a pursuit?

Pursuing the fear of the Lord is very much like pursuing the Holy Spirit. Isaiah 11:1–5 identifies the seven Spirits of God,

> "There shall come forth a Rod from the stem of Jesse, And a Branch shall grow out of his roots. The Spirit of the LORD shall rest upon Him, The Spirit of wisdom and understanding, The Spirit of counsel and might, The Spirit of knowledge and of the fear of the LORD. His delight is in the fear of the LORD, And He shall not judge by the sight of His eyes, Nor decide by the hearing of His ears; But with righteousness He shall judge the poor, And decide with equity for the meek of the earth; He shall strike the earth with the rod of His mouth, And with the breath of His lips He shall slay the wicked. Righteousness shall be the belt of His loins, And faithfulness the belt of His waist."

Three successive chapters in Revelation refer to the seven Spirits of God. Revelation 3:1 states,

> "And to the angel of the church in Sardis write, 'These things says He who has the seven Spirits of God and the seven stars; "I know your works, that you have a name that you are alive, but you are dead."'"

It is obvious from this passage that Jesus has the seven Spirits of God and is not keeping them to Himself. They are mentioned here for the purpose of alerting the church to what God has made available. Revelation 4:5 comments,

> "And from the throne proceeded lightnings, thunderings, and voices. And there were seven lamps of fire burning before the throne, which are the seven Spirits of God."

The seven Spirits of God are aflame before the throne continually. If they are aflame before the throne continually then this flame is to be caught and if it is to be caught then it can be imparted. God may want us to have this flame more than we want it, or certainly more than we want the repercussions when the fire starts burning in our lives. Revelation has one more comment about the seven Spirits in chapter 5:6,

> "And I looked, and behold, in the midst of the throne and of the four living creatures, and in the midst of the elders, stood a Lamb as though it had been slain, having seven horns and seven eyes, which are the seven Spirits of God sent out into all the earth."

Just like the church has been sent to make disciples asking God for nations fulfilling end-time prophecy, these seven Spirits don't just burn before the throne but they have been sent to help us. There is only one reason why they were sent. They were sent to empower the church. If they have been sent, then they can be possessed. They can be caught. If they can be possessed and caught, then they can be imparted. All who have received the Holy Spirit have access to these Seven. Paul specifically used that impartation to persuade men. The Spirit of the fear of the Lord releases an anointing. All who are touched by this anointing experience the fear of the Lord. Just as we pursue the Holy Spirit for His purposes, we can pursue the manifestation of the fear of the Lord. How can we persuade men if we do not have this Spirit in manifestation in our lives? Isn't that the purpose for which it was sent? It certainly seems that Paul thought so. Is it possible that possessing the fear of the Lord is as simple as asking God for this spiritual anointing?

How can we prepare to receive the spirit of the fear of the Lord? Second Corinthians 6:15–17 gives us some really good hints:

> "And what accord has Christ with Belial? Or what part has a believer with an unbeliever? And what agreement has the temple of God with idols? For you are the temple of the living God. As God has said: 'I will dwell in them and walk among them. I will be their God, and they shall be My people.' Therefore 'Come out from among them and be separate, says the Lord. Do not touch what is unclean, and I will receive you.'"

How do we prepare when we're asking God for the Spirit of the **fear of the Lord?** Part of that preparation includes a "separation" from what is worldly. By "not touching what is unclean" God says, "I will receive you." How can we ask God for an impartation of His Spirit while making covenants with death? Scripture encourages us to come out from what is unclean in order to receive divine blessing. If we're going to ask for the Spirit of the fear of the Lord, we better understand that separation **IS** the preparation. God promises to receive us in such a place.

In Second Corinthians 6:18–7:1 we are told:

> "'I will be a Father to you. And you shall be My sons and daughters, Says the LORD Almighty.' Therefore, having these promises, beloved, let us cleanse ourselves from all filthiness of the flesh and **spirit**, perfecting holiness in the fear of God."

Isn't it interesting how this is presented? Preparing for what is coming includes separating from the world and "perfecting holiness in the fear of God." Can holiness thrive in the church without the fear of the Lord? Apparently it can not. The American church seems to have been baptized in carnality, which is not good soil for holiness and the fear of the Lord. If we will prepare, God will come and do the rest. Our part is the preparation. God is ready to impart. **Our nation is desperate for it.**

What was the source of Paul's "terror of the Lord that persuades men" in Second Corinthians 5:9–11? Did Paul's terror come from being knocked off his donkey when he met Jesus? How much of God's terror did Paul learn that we don't know about? The terror of the Lord must come *to* us, before it can flow *through* us. We see it flowing through Paul very freely. In First Corinthians 5:1–3 we have such an event:

> "It is actually reported that there is sexual immorality among you, and such sexual immorality as is not even named among the Gentiles—that a man has his father's wife! And you are puffed up, and have not rather mourned, that he who has done this deed might be taken away from among you. For I indeed, as absent in body but present in spirit, have already judged, as though I were present, concerning him who has so done this deed."

How long would people living in sexual immorality feel comfortable where we go to church? How long would they be able to attend without having their specific sin or sexual addiction confronted? Can we imagine confronting this issue in a public manner? How long would it take to discern this activity in our midst? Sexual sin was apparently as widespread in Corinth as it is in our culture today, therefore the church did not hesitate to confront this issue. They understood its ability to hinder the entire congregation.

When the Spirit of the fear of the Lord is present, hostile defiling spirits are confronted and often manifest. Because Paul experienced the fear of the Lord, he didn't hesitate to confront, knowing the power was there to change the situation. How would we respond if sexual immorality was revealed in our congregation? Verses 4–8 of First Corinthians 5 declares:

> "In the name of our Lord Jesus Christ, when you are gathered together, along with my spirit, with the power of our Lord Jesus Christ, deliver such a one to Satan for the destruction of the flesh, that his spirit may be saved in the day of the Lord Jesus. Your glorying is not good. Do you not know that a little leaven leavens the whole lump? Therefore let us keep the feast, not with old leaven, nor with the leaven of malice and wickedness, but with the unleavened bread of sincerity and truth."

Have we ever had the experience of being in a church where verses 4 and 5 have been placed in operation? Where is the fear of the Lord in the church today? Is one of the reasons why we lack the fear of the Lord because leadership has not dealt biblically with these issues? Can we imagine anyone being delivered to satan for the destruction of their flesh in a public service? Is this because there is no sexual immorality, or is it because leadership chooses a different way to deal with things? Has Hollywood made sexual sin so acceptable that hardly anyone notices? What would happen if the fear of the Lord was prevalent in our church services? Are we afraid of lawsuits?

Part of the problem might be our theology concerning sin. It has been taught, for as long as I can remember, out of John 19:29–30 that when Jesus said, "It is finished!"—sin was dealt a mortal blow and from that point on we were free from its power once we made Jesus the Lord of our life. The past fifty years we have majored in preaching salvation and the love of God to the exclusion of holiness, responsibility, discipleship, and the other primary doctrines that are listed in Hebrews 6. The general feeling is that all the judgment for sin fell on Jesus and "it is finished," therefore sin is not really a problem. All we have to do is preach salvation and the love of God and let people get saved. The problem with that reasoning is it doesn't line up with Scripture. These violators were saved. They were in church. And there was very little fear of the Lord concerning their actions. Paul drew a line based on the **"Spirit of the fear of the Lord." Are we trying to operate a church model from Acts without the authority of the early church?** As God continues restoring, the power to confront sin is an inescapable part of the package. It is coming by the Spirit!

Will we be thinking grace, grace, grace
When we shall meet Him face to face
Or will this encounter come with dread
Awed by Him as one knocked dead?

Jayne Houghton

Chapter 14

Jesus the Judge

Over two decades ago the Lord spoke something to me that dramatically changed my thinking concerning what we are going to face in the end-times. He said, "You are expecting the Jesus that Peter, James, and John got, and they were looking for the Jesus that you're going to get." I had never thought about Jesus having two distinctively different but complementary ministries. The ascension and seating at the right hand of the Father marked the completion of His saving work (salvation was fully birthed) and the beginning of Jesus the Judge, as revealed in Revelation. Scripture validates the ministry of Jesus the Judge. The Jesus that Peter, James, and John expected was the Messiah of the prophets. The suffering Servant confounded them and has continued to confound the Jews for two thousand years. The book of Revelation reveals Jesus the Judge! He is the God of the prophets and the Judge of all the earth. The Healing, Delivering, Saving Jesus, that Peter, James, and John walked with as a suffering servant, was not the One they wanted or expected. They had no eschatology for a suffering Servant and thanks to rapture teaching the church has no eschatology for "Jesus the Judge," the God of the prophets! The Jesus we can expect is described in Revelation 19:11–15,

"Then I saw heaven opened, and behold, a white horse. And He who sat on him was called Faithful and True, and in righteousness He judges and makes war. His eyes were like a flame of fire, and on His head were many crowns. He had a name written that no one knew except Himself. He was clothed with a robe dipped in blood, and His name is called The Word of God. And the armies in heaven, clothed in fine linen, white and clean, followed Him on white horses. Now out of His mouth goes a sharp sword, that with it He should strike the nations. And He Himself will rule them with a rod of iron. He Himself treads the winepress of the fierceness and wrath of Almighty God."

Are we preparing the church to walk with the God of war? Are we introducing them to the Judge of all the earth? Or have we camped out in the Gospels where Jesus is Savior, Healer, Baptizer in the Holy Spirit, and Deliverer!? Does the church know the Jesus who is about to manifest in our midst? Are we preparing congregations for what they are about to witness? If Jesus the Judge would show up in our church on Sunday morning, how would we react? Disciples should be fully comfortable with Jesus the Judge, but His manifestation would probably shock the "Hell" out of converts! The fear of the Lord catapulted forward in the early church after Jesus the Judge manifested.

In Revelation chapters 2 and 3, Jesus came to seven different churches as the Judge of all the earth. To the church at Ephesus He said, "Nevertheless I have this against you, that you have left your first love." Retranslated for the American church, "you have settled for converts and have not gone on to make disciples." In verse 5, He said to Ephesus:

"Remember therefore from where you have fallen, repent and do

> the first works, or else I will come to you quickly and remove your lampstand from its place—unless you repent."

When Jesus the Judge revealed Himself to the church in Ephesus, He said, "If you want to save your anointing, if you want to keep your lampstand, if you want to keep your gifting and calling, then you need to make some changes. You need to go back to your first love. Don't run to evangelical theology thinking it will save you. Pentecostal theology offers the same trap. Following the Holy Spirit is the only answer." If we don't pay attention, our lampstand may be removed. How is the lampstand in the church where we attend? Is it burning bright? Or is it burning dim? Jesus is coming to visit but will the following define the visitation? Malachi 3:1–2:

> "'Behold I send My messenger, And he will prepare the way before Me. And the Lord, whom you seek, Will suddenly come to His temple, Even the Messenger of the covenant, In whom you delight. Behold, He is coming,' says the LORD of hosts. But who can endure the day of His coming? And who can stand when He appears? For He is like a refiner's fire And like fuller's soap."

Jesus revealed Himself as a Judge to the Ephesians.

In Revelation 2:14–16, writing to the church at Pergamos, Jesus said:

> "But I have a few things against you, because you have there those who hold the doctrine of Balaam; who taught Balak to put a stumbling block before the children of Israel, to eat things sacrificed to idols, and to commit sexual immorality. Thus you also have those who hold the doctrine of the Nicolaitans, which

> thing I hate. Repent, or else I will come to you quickly and will fight against them with the sword of My mouth."

The Jesus who visits the church in Pergamos says, "I will come to you quickly and will fight against them with the sword of My mouth." I thought Jesus was supposed to be fighting ***for*** us? What if we find Jesus fighting ***against*** us? Is it because there is something we need to change? Pergamos needed change. Is our church doing what Jesus called us to do? Are we preparing people for the manifestation of His presence? Or are we safely camped out in the Gospels, occasionally wandering into the book of Acts? What are we preparing for? Do we expect to be raptured out, or to walk through? Are we willing to be the mouth and hands of Jesus in the earth, speaking things people don't like to hear? What are we preparing for? How many of us know the Jesus of Ananias and Sapphira?

In Revelation 2:21–22, speaking to the church in Thyatira, Jesus said this:

> "And I gave her time to repent of her sexual immorality, and she did not repent. Indeed I will cast her into a sickbed, and those who commit adultery with her into **great tribulation**, unless they repent of their deeds."

I thought Jesus was suppose to be our Healer. But here, He says, for sexual immorality and adultery, He brings "**sickness and great tribulation**. . . ." Not everybody who faces sickness and tribulation is facing it because of immorality—that is obvious. These things need to be discerned. Sometimes we face it because the Lord is using us as Romans 8 describes, sheep led to the slaughter in order to birth an anointing to destroy the enemy in a certain area. The issue in Revelation is that suddenly we see the contrast between Jesus the Savior and Jesus the Judge! Jesus in Revelation is quite different from Jesus in the Gospels. He is different because in Revelation He is Judge of all the earth. Why is it that Paul could decree blindness on the false prophet in Acts 13 and we often stand before the enemy impotent? If Paul had not known the ascended, seated-at-the-right-hand Jesus the Judge, he could never have decreed judgment. If we're not preparing a generation to walk with Jesus the Judge, we are forfeiting future giftings and callings. The church can not believe for what it doesn't understand.

In Revelation 3:3, writing to the church at Sardis, Jesus said:

> "Remember therefore how you have received and heard; hold fast and repent. Therefore if you will not watch, I will come upon you as a thief, and you will not know what hour I will come upon you."

What happens if we don't go on to complete the assignments Jesus calls us to do? We enter a prophetic blindness where we misjudge the times and seasons and cannot recognize Him when He comes. To such people, Jesus promised to appear as a thief, taking away what they should have possessed. When Jesus visits the churches of Revelation, He comes as Jesus the Judge. Are we ready for a visit from this Jesus? Are the people who attend our churches ready? The fear of the Lord is coming.

Writing to the church at Laodicea, Jesus said in Revelation 3:15–16:

> "I know your works, that you are neither cold nor hot. I could wish you were cold or hot. So then, because you are lukewarm, and neither cold nor hot, I will spew you out of My mouth."

Jesus the Judge dispenses customized judgments which reflect the sin. I would not want to be responsible for a parishioner's lukewarmness. How would you like to give an account, if you had a ministry, for allowing people to be lukewarm? That would be hard. Do we know Jesus the Judge? Are we prepared to walk with Him in the last days? To walk with Him also means to announce or dispense His judgment. Do the often treasonous, traitorous, and usually perverse works of Hollywood—spewing "blame America first" propaganda—need Jesus the Judge? Does the United States Senate need Jesus the Judge? Do we need Jesus the Judge to visit the Supreme Court? Who is going to bring Him forth except the c-h-u-r-c-h?

Is it any wonder we don't have any **fear of the Lord** in Hollywood? Is it any wonder we don't have the **fear of the Lord** in the Senate? There is very little in the church. We have the same level of the fear of the Lord in Hollywood, in the Senate, in the House of Representatives, and in the Supreme Court as we have in the church! Only the restoration of the fear of the Lord can impact Senators enough to pass a Federal Marriage Amendment. Only the fear of the Lord can turn bastard judges into honorable men who think straight. No man can live crooked and think straight. The **fear of the Lord** has to start in the church!

How awesome is the God of strength
Of power and majesty
The mighty Judge of all the earth
A Man of war is He

His purity and holiness
Demands utmost respect
Are we prepared such power to meet
And with Him intersect?

Jayne Houghton

Chapter 15

Physical Israel and the Fear of the Lord

Physical Israel presents a wonderful opportunity for the church. For the theologically rigid it is much more an issue of debate and division than, in my estimation, it ever should have been. The timing has special significance for those of us that were born prior to Jerusalem being returned to full control of the Jews after the 1967 Six-Day War. Jesus prophesied concerning this season in Luke 21:24:

> "And they will fall by the edge of the sword, and be led away captive into all nations. And Jerusalem will be trampled by Gentiles until the times of the Gentiles are fulfilled."

The Six-Day War of 1967 marked the fulfillment of Jesus words. The time of the Gentiles being fulfilled apparently means that we are coming into the season where the church has the assignment of grafting Israel back in to God's vine and possessing the anointing to make them jealous. When the church could be agreeing about God's purpose for us and seeking the ultimate restoration of resurrection power, we find ourselves in some pharisaical circles debating and dividing over the phrase "Replacement Theology." It seems to me even the phrase is ridiculous, because if the New Covenant didn't fulfill and in some instances replace actions required under the Old Covenant then every believer must travel to Jerusalem and offer a sacrifice for sin once a year. The phrase "Replacement Theology" may have its origin in satan himself. This is a season for the church to come into unity and harmony based on one of our emerging prophetic purposes, which is dramatically explained in Romans. We will answer to God for discipling a generation who are called to graft Israel back into the vine. The church, as the body of Christ, has to fulfill Bible prophecy.

Ephesians chapter 2:11–14 states:

> "Therefore remember that you, once Gentiles in the flesh—who are called Uncircumcision by what is called the Circumcision made in the flesh by hands—that at that time you were without Christ, being aliens from the commonwealth of Israel and strangers from the covenants of promise, having no hope and without God in the world. But now in Christ Jesus you who once were far off have been made near by the blood of Christ. For He Himself is our peace, who has made **both** (Jew and Gentile) one, and has broken down the middle wall of division between us."

The New Covenant makes it clear that Jesus merged Jew and Gentile into **one new man.** There is only one way for either Jew or Gentile to become a **new man**—we must be born again. Any born-again believer is more Jewish than any physical Jew who hasn't met Messiah.

In Romans 9:1–5 Paul specifically laments the condition of physical Israel saying that he wishes he could be blotted out or "accursed from Christ for my brethren . . . according to the flesh" so they could be grafted in. Verses 6–8 are quite enlightening in the context of his heartfelt intercession for physical Israel:

> "But it is not that the word of God has taken no effect. For they are not all Israel who are of Israel, nor are they all children because they are the seed of Abraham; but, 'In Isaac your seed shall be called.' That is, those who are the children of the flesh, these are not the children of God; but the children of the promise are counted as the seed."

Who are the "children of God"? Who is counted as the "seed of Abraham"? Who are the children of the flesh and who are the children of promise? Paul made that very clear. How could it be **more clearly** stated than, "For they are not all Israel who are of Israel"? In Romans 2:26–29 Paul had already addressed this issue:

> "Therefore, if any uncircumcised man keeps the righteous requirements of the law, will not his uncircumcision be counted as circumcision? And will not the physically uncircumcised, if he fulfills the law, judge you who, even with your written code and circumcision, are a transgressor of the law? For he is not a Jew who is one outwardly, nor is that circumcision which is outward in the flesh; but he is a Jew who is one inwardly, and circumcision is that of the heart, in the Spirit, and not in the letter; whose praise is not from men but from God."

Paul defines a Jew as a doer of the word and he who is not a Jew simply rejects doing God's word. To Paul, the physical Israel of today would not yet have become Jewish.

In Galatians 4, Paul was very concerned about all the believers who were trying to go back and become Jewish, by embracing all the ordinances, not realizing that by faith they already were. He said in verses 19–21:

> "My little children, for whom I **labor in birth again until Christ is formed in you**, I would like to be present with you now and to change my tone; for I have doubts about you. Tell me, you who desire to be under the law, do you not hear the law?"

Paul goes on to say, in verses 22–26, exactly where things stand for the church:

> "For it is written that Abraham had two sons: the one by a bondwoman, the other by a freewoman. But he who was of the bondwoman was born according to the flesh, and he of the freewoman through promise, which things are symbolic. For these are the two covenants: the one from Mount Sinai which gives birth to bondage, which is Hagar—for this Hagar is Mount Sinai in Arabia, and corresponds to **Jerusalem which now is**, and is in bondage with her children—but the Jerusalem above is free, which is the mother of us all."

To be in the church is to be Jewish and have full access to the covenants of Promise. We are part of the Israel of God and we have a Jerusalem and our Jerusalem is not in the Middle East. Our Jerusalem is free. Our Jerusalem is above. The one in the Middle East is in bondage. Those who occupy Jerusalem in physical Israel have to find their Messiah and join us as occupants of the New Jerusalem.

The apostle John wrote the book of Revelation and apparently he had the very same understanding. In Revelation 11, speaking of the two witnesses, he says in verses 7–8:

> "Now when they finish their testimony, the beast that ascends out of the bottomless pit will make war against them, overcome them, and kill them. And their dead bodies will lie in the street of the great city which spiritually is called **Sodom and Egypt,** where also our Lord was crucified."

John called the Jerusalem which still exists today "Sodom and Egypt. . . ." That understanding makes praying for the peace of Jerusalem an exercise in spiritual futility. Does God love the physical Jew? God's heart for the Jew is beyond loving them. He gives the church an assignment in Romans chapter 11 that we have to embrace. In Romans 11:1–2 Paul says that God has *not* cast away physical Israel. He says:

> "I say then, has God cast away His people? Certainly not! For I also am an Israelite, of the seed of Abraham, of the tribe of Benjamin. God has not cast away His people whom He foreknew. Or do you not know what the Scripture says of Elijah, how he pleads with God against Israel, saying. . . ."

Verses 11–15 give us a picture of the anointing we have to birth and pass on to a generation in order that they may graft physical Israel back in to the vine. Paul said:

> "I say then, have they stumbled that they should fall? Certainly not! But through their fall, to provoke them to jealousy, salvation has come to the Gentiles. Now if their fall is riches for the world, and their failure riches for the Gentiles, how much more **their fullness**! For I speak to you Gentiles; inasmuch as I am an apostle to the Gentiles, I magnify my ministry, if by any means I may provoke to jealousy those who are my flesh and save some of them. For if their being cast away is the reconciling of the world, what

will their acceptance be but life from the dead?" (Resurrection power cometh in great measure for this divine purpose.)

If those of us in the church want to see the resurrection power flowing consistently with miracles, great signs, and wonders, then it appears in Paul's prophetic understanding that grafting Israel back in to the church releases that anointing, beyond anything else we could do. Demons develop division, usually over theology. How can we graft Israel back in without the **fear of the Lord?** Notice verses 19–24:

> "You will say then, 'Branches were broken off that I might be grafted in.' Well said. Because of unbelief they were broken off, and you stand by faith. Do not be haughty, **but fear**. For if God did not spare the natural branches, He may not spare you either. Therefore **consider the goodness and severity of God**: on those who fell, severity; but toward you, goodness, if you continue in His goodness. Otherwise you also will be cut off. And they also, if they do not continue in unbelief, will be grafted in, **for God is able to graft them in again**. For if you were cut out of the olive tree which is wild by nature, and were grafted contrary to nature into a good olive tree, how much more will these, who are the natural branches, be grafted into their own olive tree?"

Verse 20 makes it very clear that the church is to look at the current condition of physical Israel as a source of the fear of the Lord. The spirit of Antichrist is alive and well, ruling over physical Israel. But we, the church, have a prophetic assignment. Physical Israel has to become Jewish by being born again, or we have to apply a pen knife cutting Ephesians 2 out of the New Testament. They are currently bound in their religious tradition and as spiritually blind as a goose in a snow storm. We are to look at them and "consider the goodness and severity of God." It is to produce the fear of the Lord for the church. And God promises an anointing for the church that will graft Israel back into the vine.

In verses 25–28 Paul says:

> "For I do not desire, brethren, that you should be ignorant of this mystery, lest you should be wise in your own opinion, that hardening in part has happened to Israel until the fullness of the Gentiles has come in. And so all Israel will be saved, as it is written: 'The Deliverer will come out of Zion, And He will turn away ungodliness from Jacob; For this is My covenant with them, When I take away their sins.' Concerning the gospel they are enemies for your sake, but concerning the election they are beloved for the sake of the fathers."

Physical Israel has a covenantal prophetic promise because of the fathers, not because of anything they are doing right now. The greatest reservoir of the spirit of Antichrist I've ever experienced outside of Hollywood exists in Israel, making the ministry of the Gospel quite difficult. The magnitude of the spirit of Antichrist can be seen in the ACLU which is dedicated to removing everything Christian from America, even symbols like the cross. The ACLU is primarily staffed by Jewish attorneys. But God has promised to graft them back in and lift the blinders. The **fear of the Lord** is a major element in that process. How can we embrace God's prophetic purpose for the church, if we don't look at physical Israel and their condition as a source releasing the fear of the Lord? Paul went on to say in verses 29–32:

> "For the gifts and the calling of God are irrevocable. For as you were once disobedient to God, yet have now obtained mercy

through their disobedience, even so these also have now been disobedient, that **through the mercy shown you, they also may obtain mercy.** For God has committed them all to disobedience, that He might have mercy on all."

I read, ". . . through the mercy shown you, they also may obtain mercy" to mean physical Israel gets grafted back into the vine through the church.

"For the gifts and the callings of God are irrevocable." I believe we have an assignment to disciple a generation who knows prophetically that God is going to graft physical Israel back into the vine through the church, and this generation is going to walk in such power as to cause the Jewish people great jealousy. How can we prepare for that? We certainly have to ask for the **fear of the Lord,** but Paul leaves us with the issue of mercy as a foundational principle upon which all these other things will manifest.

It is time to stop debating the stupidity of "Replacement Theology" and recognize division comes from the devil. A good friend, who I was ordained with and greatly respect after twenty years on the mission field followed by ten years pastoring, said of "Replacement Theology," "Let's face it, all these slogans are a futile attempt to maintain dispensationalism intact especially the pre-tribulation rapture." It is time to embrace the prophetic purpose of God which is grafting the Jew back in through the fear of the Lord and the power of the Spirit. This is a subject of such width and breadth that it deserves a much greater depth of treatment than is presented here. This chapter is a plea for unity over one of God's pinnacle church assignments, grafting the physical Jew back into the vine!

Grafting God's family
  Back into the vine
One new man
    Partaking of the Divine

Both Gentile and Jew
    Came together as **One**
Following the Father
    Proclaiming the **Son**

Jayne Houghton

Chapter 16

The Covenant of Sure Mercy

It seems the fastest preparational path for birthing an anointing to make the physical Jew jealous is to immerse ourselves in the covenant of sure mercy. Isaiah 55:1–3 extends this covenant to everyone who thirsts:

> "Ho! Everyone who thirsts, Come to the waters; And you who have no money, Come buy and eat. Yes, come, buy wine and milk Without money and without price. Why do you spend money for what is not bread, And your wages for what does not satisfy? Listen diligently to Me, and eat what is good, And let your soul delight itself in abundance. Incline your ear, and come to Me. Hear, and your soul shall live; And I will make an everlasting covenant with you—The sure mercies of David."

God promises the extension of the Davidic covenant to all believers. He says all we have to do is be hungry and come to Him. If we're thirsty, it's available. He will make an everlasting covenant with us, even the sure mercies of David. God extends a covenant of mercy to us so that we might, in His behalf, truly extend it individually, corporately, regionally, and nationally. Psalm 2 has to be fulfilled. "Ask of Me, and I will give You the nations. . . ." The covenant of sure mercy is the foundation for fulfilling Psalm 2. What is the covenant of sure mercy and where did God first extend it?

Second Samuel 7:1–7 describes the atmosphere in which the covenant of sure mercy was offered to David. Verses 1–6 say:

> "Now it came to pass when the king was dwelling in his house, and the LORD had given him rest from all his enemies all around, that the king said to Nathan the prophet, 'See now, I dwell in a house of cedar, but the ark of God dwells inside tent curtains.' Then Nathan said to the king, 'Go, do all that is in your heart, for the LORD is with you.' But it happened that night that the word of the LORD came to Nathan, saying, 'Go and tell My servant David, "Thus says the LORD: 'Would you build a house for Me to dwell in? For I have not dwelt in a house since the time that I brought the children of Israel up from Egypt, even to this day, but have moved about in a tent and in a tabernacle.'""

David wanted to build God a house because the Ark of Israel was in tent curtains. It was God's idea to build David a house. God's purpose for David could not be fulfilled if sin disqualified him like it had Saul. The covenant of sure mercy guaranteed a Kingdom contribution consistent with his gifting and calling, even if he had a moral failure. Saul's failure ended his reign and right of succession. Only a covenant of sure mercy could prevent a reoccurrence. Each of us need the assurance we can make an eternal contribution—without the fear of disqualification through personal failure.

Second Samuel 7:7–15 describes the actual covenant:

> "In all the places where I have walked with all the children of Israel, have I ever spoken a word to anyone from the tribes of Israel, whom I commanded to shepherd My people Israel, saying, 'Why have you not built Me a house of cedar?' Now therefore, thus shall you say to My servant David, 'Thus says the LORD of hosts: I took you from the sheepfold, from following the sheep, to be ruler over My people, over Israel, And I have been with you wherever you have gone, and have cut off all your enemies from before you, and have made you a great name, like the name of the great men who are on the earth. Moreover I will appoint a place for My people Israel, and will plant them, that they may dwell in a place of their own and move no more; nor shall the sons of wickedness oppress them anymore, as previously, since the time that I commanded judges to be over My people Israel, and have caused you to rest from all your enemies. Also the LORD tells you that He will make you a house. When your days are fulfilled and you rest with your fathers, I will set up your seed after you, who will come from your body, and I will establish his kingdom. He shall build a house for My name, and I will establish the throne of his kingdom forever. I will be his Father, and he shall be My son. If he commits iniquity, I will chasten him with the rod of men and with the blows of the sons of men. But My mercy shall not depart from him, as I took it from Saul, whom I removed from before you.'"

The essence of this covenant is God's desire to not take His mercy from David and his son as He took it from Saul. The reason for the covenant of mercy is **establishing** the work of David's hands and the **work** of his son's hands. That work is consistent as a type and shadow of the work we are called to do today. David and his son were embarking on the task of preparing for and building the temple of God in the natural. Our call is to build an eternal spiritual temple made up of eternal living stones. For most of us, without the covenant of mercy, the work of our hands could not be established if we experienced a moral failure. Because of man's propensity to fail, God extended a covenant of sure mercy allowing Him to establish the work of our hands in any generation, even if we commit a disqualifying sin. That makes God the ultimate restorer and redeemer of failures! He covenants with us to redeem our crooked places but demands that we in turn redeem others. Birthing an anointing that impacts a nation requires that we extend mercy and redemption without judging and disqualifying those who seem fatally flawed. We must begin to embrace the covenant of mercy in more than understanding because we have to demonstrate it in practice.

The question arises, What exactly does God mean when He says, "But My mercy shall not depart from him as I took it from Saul, whom I removed from before you"? First Samuel 15 records the removal of mercy from Saul and gives us some insight into God's heart concerning war. As various issues arise and are debated in American politics, no issue brings greater controversy to the church than war! We have seen signs saying "What would Jesus do?" "Who would Jesus bomb?" or "Would Jesus go to war?" Whenever I see such displays, I am always struck with the unbelievable display of biblical ignorance alerting the whole world to the fact they obviously don't know God and certainly don't know His Son! Jesus is the same yesterday today and forever. Therefore, He is no different than what we view in First Samuel 15:1–3:

> "Samuel also said to Saul, 'The Lord sent me to anoint you king over His people, over Israel. Now therefore, heed the voice of the words of the Lord.' Thus says the Lord of hosts: 'I will punish what Amalek did to Israel, how he laid wait for him on the way when he came up from Egypt. Now go and attack Amalek, and

> utterly destroy all that they have, and do not spare them. But kill both man and woman, infant and nursing child, ox and sheep, camel and donkey.'"

When God goes to war, He "nukes 'em." God commanded Saul to, "kill both man and woman, infant and nursing child, ox and sheep, camel and donkey." It doesn't appear that anything was to be left alive. Why would God do that? That certainly doesn't fit the "politically correct" milk-toast Jesus often presented by today's media. When Israel spent 400 years in Egypt and God brought them out, they did not know war. They did not know God as a warrior. They *learned* about God the warrior, His judgment and His justice when they saw the Egyptians dead upon the sea shore. Exodus 15:1–3 reveals God as a warrior:

> "Then Moses and the children of Israel sang this song to the LORD, and spoke, saying: 'I will sing to the LORD, For He has triumphed gloriously! The horse and its rider He has thrown into the sea! The LORD is my strength and song, And He has become my salvation; He is my God, and I will praise Him; My father's God, and I will exalt Him. **The LORD is a man of war**; The LORD is His name.'"

They learned that the LORD was a man of war and when God went to war He did not limit His attack. He did not make the common distinctions that are made today. When God went to war, you knew it and you knew when it was over! The Bible says we have to renew our mind to *know* Him. Isaiah 42:13 also reveals this nature of God:

> "The LORD shall go forth like a mighty man; He shall stir up His zeal like a man of war. He shall cry out, yes, shout aloud; He shall prevail against His enemies."

We usually find people who are willing to offer the caveat that all those Old Testament verses don't really apply since Jesus came and died for everybody. But Revelation 19:11–15 reveals those arguments for the fertilizer they really are:

> "Then I saw heaven opened, and behold, a white horse. And He who sat on him was called Faithful and True; and in righteousness He judges and makes war. His eyes were like a flame of fire, and on His head were many crowns. He had a name written that no one knew except Himself. He was clothed with a robe dipped in blood, and His name is called The Word of God. And the armies in heaven, clothed in fine linen, white and clean, followed Him on white horses. Now out of His mouth goes a sharp sword, that with it He should strike the nations. And He Himself will rule them with a rod of iron. He Himself treads the winepress of the fierceness and wrath of Almighty God."

Jesus is the "man of war" of Exodus 15 and Isaiah 42. He is the same yesterday, today, and forever! He is the One who is returning. He is the One that the church has to represent as we prepare for the last days. Do we know the God of war?

Much has been made of Jesus' admonition to "turn the other cheek," but when we place those remarks in context there is a far different application than the anti-war lunacy often claimed. The Sermon on the Mount was directed to believers about their conduct within a believing community. The subject of war and responding to national enemies is well covered in the New Testament from Romans to Revelation. Romans 13:1–4 says,

> "Let every soul be subject to the governing authorities. For there is no authority except from God, and the authorities that exist are appointed by God. Therefore whoever resists the authority resists

> the ordinance of God, and those who resist will bring judgment on themselves. For rulers are not a terror to good works, but to evil. Do you want to be unafraid of the authority? Do what is good, and you will have praise from the same. For he is God's minister to you for good. But if you do evil, be afraid; for he does not bear the sword in vain; for he is God's minister, an avenger to execute wrath on him who practices evil."

Government is God's minister and as such has a divine calling to kill and destroy enemies who practice evil. Joining the military is a very godly honorable courageous thing to do. Bible-believing Christians should be the greatest warriors on earth. Claiming Christian faith as the foundation for pacifism is cowardly heresy! The God of the Bible anointed Moses to kill the entire Egyptian army. Joshua needed more daylight to kill the enemy and God stopped the rotation of the universe for nearly a whole day to help him! In Isaiah 37, Hezekiah prayed against the enemy and God sent an angel to kill 185,000 Assyrians. That angel is still available and familiar with the region. God anointed David to kill thousands and allowed David to covenant with others who became "mighty men" where one could kill a thousand and two could dispatch ten thousand. If the resurrected Christ didn't hesitate to kill Ananias and Sapphira for not telling the truth, why would He hesitate anointing us to destroy demonized terrorists? Jesus is a **"man of war"** and we better get to ***know*** **Him!**

One of America's great generals during World War I is reported to have answered a soldier's objection to killing the enemy, having heard some of them were Christians. A soldier asked, "What if some of the enemy are Christians, like us?" The general's response was quick and to the point, "Kill 'em all and let God sort it out." That view certainly reflects the God of war that we find in First Samuel 15.

The penalty for Saul's refusal to destroy all men, women, children, and animals was losing the three most valuable things that God had given him. Verse 11 of First Samuel 15 records God's heart over the issue:

> "'I greatly regret that I have set up Saul as king, for he has turned back from following Me, and has not performed My commandments.' And it grieved Samuel, and he cried out to the LORD all night."

In verses 22 and 23 Saul lost his office. He was rejected from being king. In verse 26 we have the addition of two words that are different from the last part of verse 23. In verse 23 we are told, "He also has rejected you from being king," while verse 26 says, "And the LORD has rejected you from being king **over Israel**." The first thing Saul lost was his **office.** The second thing he lost was his **call.** The difference is in the addition of the words, "**over Israel**." Being king is the office. "Over Israel" is the call. David lost his office when he had to flee from Absalom. He did not, however, lose the call, and regained the office and finished his divine assignment, appropriating the covenant of sure mercy. It was *not* due to the fact that he had not qualified for removal, just as Saul had. The difference was David had a covenant. Every office and call demand a corresponding anointing to fulfill them.

Saul's third penalty was losing the anointing to walk in the office and fulfill the call. When God sent Samuel to anoint another in Saul's place, as the Spirit of God came upon the replacement, He departed from Saul. First Samuel 16:13–14 states:

> "Then Samuel took the horn of oil and anointed him in the midst of his brothers; and the Spirit of the LORD said, 'Arise, anoint him;

for this is the one!' But the Spirit of the LORD departed from Saul, and a distressing spirit from the LORD troubled him."

Saul lost the anointing to walk in the office and fulfill the call. He was given over to distress and trouble. The third portion of the penalty was the worst of all. All discernment disappeared. From this point on, he would consistently war against God's purpose and against the anointing on David's life. This tragic end could have been avoided had Saul been obedient by killing everyone and destroying everything! Saul lost it all in a moment of unsanctified mercy. The attitude against war propagated by the media, pseudo-intellectuals, college professors, and championed by the liberal left may, if successful, turn America into a Saul who loses everything! Is Jesus still the same yesterday, today, and forever when it comes to war? According to the book of Revelation, Jesus is every bit the same as the God who took all from Saul for not executing the people of Ammon. When we face a demonized terrorist culture today, if we go to war, we should go with a biblical mindset.

The covenant of sure mercy says when you have a moral failure, you don't have to lose your office, you don't have to lose the call, and you don't have to lose the anointing of the Holy Spirit to walk in the office and fulfill the call. In the Kingdom the work of our hands can be established in building God's purposes even if we have a failure. If failure disqualified us from our personal contribution, the Kingdom would never be built! The real issue for the church concerning the covenant of sure mercy is how do we treat people in failure? Do we work to restore them or do we banish them and send them off on their merry way more wounded than they ever were prior to the failure?

God's heart for restoration will judge us. Are we working *with* Him or are we working *against* Him? David had a failure that paralleled Saul's. Some, I suppose, could argue that David's failure was actually worse than Saul's. Saul refused to kill everybody. He was in failure because of disobedience. David started out with adultery but ended in murder. What can we say about that? Saul lost his kingship for *not* killing people and animals. David deserved to lose his *for* shedding innocent blood. If we were to judge that in the natural, we would have to say that David's failure was significantly worse than Saul's. But we can't do that. We have to judge it by Scripture. What is the difference between the two men? One had a covenant of sure mercy. The other did not. David deserved to lose everything, but instead he set the example of how to respond to God in failure when we have a covenant of mercy.

The very first thing David did was appeal to that covenant. Is that the first thing that happens to us when we discover a brother or sister in major moral failure? Do we reach for the covenant of sure mercy? Or do we reach for the sword of God's word to separate them through judgment? End-time preparation means we have to embrace and practice the covenant of sure mercy.

Second Samuel 12:9–14 records David's confrontation and response:

> "Why have you despised the commandment of the LORD, to do evil in His sight? You have killed Uriah the Hittite with the sword; you have taken his wife to be your wife, and have killed him with the sword of the people of Ammon. Now therefore, the sword shall never depart from your house, because you have despised Me, and have taken the wife of Uriah the Hittite to be your wife. Thus says the LORD: 'Behold, I will raise up adversity against you from your own house; and I will take your wives before your eyes and give them to your neighbor, and he shall lie with your

> wives in the sight of this sun. For you did it secretly, but I will do this thing before all Israel, before the sun.' Then David said to Nathan, 'I have sinned against the LORD.' And Nathan said to David, 'The LORD also has put away your sin; you shall not die. However, because by this deed you have given great occasion to the enemies of the LORD to blaspheme, the child also who is born to you shall surely die.'"

What things are within the boundaries of the covenant of sure mercy and what things reside outside these boundaries? This covenant does not remove the circumstances or the biblical judgments that accompany the sins we commit. It does bring forgiveness and restore our relationship with God. It does guarantee that we can continue in our office, in our call, and not lose the anointing of the Holy Spirit. But let us be quick to point out that David spent the rest of his life dealing with the sword in his own family. God's judgment for his sin was that the sword never departed. Are there good reasons why we should not sin? David can identify all of them. Is the covenant of sure mercy awesome? It is! It allows us to complete God's call on our life. But it doesn't mean that we escape the personal pain and agony of our failures. There is a reason why we should avoid sin. It does have a penalty that can last a lifetime, nevertheless God offers redemption and forgiveness for the sin. He offers restoration of relationship. And He offers to take us on from that point and give us a productive life where we can fulfill the call that is ours. Only God can redeem failure and turn it to a platform for our greatest success.

There's a foundational covenant
The mercy there is sure
Mistakes and failures God transforms
Forgiveness is secure

This redemptive covenant
Blesses individually
Be aware it acts, as well,
Corporate and nationally

Jayne Houghton

Chapter 17

Eight Steps of Restoration

Second Samuel 12:13–14 records steps one and two.

> "Then David said to Nathan, 'I have sinned against the LORD.' And Nathan said to David, 'The LORD also has put away your sin; you shall not die. However, because by this deed you have given great occasion to the enemies of the LORD to blaspheme, the child also who is born to you shall surely die.'"

In step one David acknowledges his sin. Restoration can never occur if the perpetrating party refuses to open the primary passageway. Acknowledging or "owning our stuff" is an act of transparency and humility which God requires. A failure to acknowledge ends all hope of restoration. In step two the offending party accepts the righteous judgment and restoration plan as outlined by those to whom he has submitted.

Verse 20 records step three as a personal choice to arise in the midst of failure. Every person must choose to get up and transition from the position of mourning over their failure to accepting God's forgiveness. This means acting on what Jesus' blood bought.

David had to choose to get up. No one could pick him up. This is something that has to register in the heart. We must help people through the devastation of what their sin has produced with an attitude reflecting grace and forgiveness. Many choose to live in the paralysis of the past. The apostle Paul tells us in Philippians that "forgetting the things that are behind we choose to press on toward the upper call of God in Christ Jesus." Oftentimes we have to reach out to those in failure with that attitude. It is time to see God arise over His people, and to be the agents of restoration. This is the function of mercy. It has a most practical application. We become the hands, heart, and words of God extended to those in failure, enabling them to arise.

Step number four is also in verse 20. David makes the choice to wash. Washing is the process necessary of cleansing the conscience, enabling the individual to pick up God's call once again. The conscience has to be washed of all the effects of the sin. Each of us have to accept the fact that righteousness is something that is God-given and relationally nurtured. It is not something we earn. Washing is absolutely essential to restore this reality. Washing cleanses self-condemnation. David washes the shame away, which is necessary in moving toward restored confidence in his gifting and calling.

The fifth step recorded in verse 20 is the choice to anoint himself. This reflects the anointing of being clean. He is returning with confidence to ministry. There are two different Hebrew words for "anointing." One is the anointing that is a one-time event which comes when a person is initiated into ministry. David answered the call when Samuel poured the anointing over his head. The anointing that David is experiencing here is not an application of the holy anointing oil. This anointing reflects the joy of being made clean and the restoration of confidence attained through God's forgiveness. It is a very important step in transformation. It is the fruit of restoration. Oftentimes people need our support in order to accomplish this washing. It is through corporate acceptance, confirmation, and encouragement of the church that this spiritual washing is completed.

The sixth step David takes in verse 20 is the changing of his clothes. This signifies putting on the kingly robes of divine authority that are appropriate to the authority of the believer. This is a step that is essential because it becomes a statement in the realm of the spirit. This act declares we have returned to the authority of our gifting and calling. We cannot do this if we are not clean or if we have not appropriated a restored sense of righteousness. A restored sense of acceptance by the body is essential in this stage. This is where the body is very necessary in completing and restoring God's purpose for the individual. David put on his kingly robes so he could once again stand in the office and fulfill the call. The same thing has to be done in the realm of the spirit for every individual who has walked through a failure.

In step seven, David returns to the house of the LORD, worships, and reconnects with God. The sin is over. The restoration is nearly complete. He can't change the past. He knows it. It is time to reconnect with the LORD and receive the boldness that comes because his sin is cleansed. David is ready. He embraces God in worship. This is the seventh step in moving back toward full restoration. Are we willing to extend this to those who fail and to those who hurt us in the process? God has revealed His heart. Now it must become our heart.

In step number eight, David has to become an agent of restoration. This is where David's history could work against him. His past experience with a woman who caused great trouble was banishment. As the king he had this authority. Apparently he exercised it concerning Michal. She was locked up and became barren, possibly because she was never allowed to see a man again. David cannot do that with Bathsheba. His affair with her brought much more reproach on his kingship than Michal's antics ever did. David had to extend the same mercy to Bathsheba that God extended to him. In the process of that extension he becomes God's heart and God's hands of mercy. What would happen if the church began to move in restoration? How would our communities react to such demonstrations? Perhaps we would gain a reputation of doing what we preach. How would the world react if the church were actually to become the agent of restoration for the failures of our society? In Isaiah 55 we are promised what God will do if we extend His covenant of sure mercy. Verses 3–5 declare, concerning David:

> "Incline your ear, and come to Me. Hear, and your soul shall live; And I will make an everlasting covenant with you—The sure mercies of David. Indeed I have given him as a witness to the people, A leader and commander for the people. Surely you shall call a nation you do not know, And nations who do not know you shall run to you, Because of the LORD your God, And the Holy One of Israel; For He has glorified you."

God promises that we shall call a nation we do not know, and nations who do not know us shall run to us, once they see the manifestation of mercy in our lives. Apparently the world is waiting to see this covenant of mercy in operation. If we can manifest it, we qualify for an anointing that will cause nations to run to us. How are we doing? Converts don't have to extend mercy. They can judge people, throw them out, put them on the sideline, banished from all leadership, never to be seen or heard again. Converts can easily judge, get mad, discontinue a relationship, forget about it, and quickly find a replacement. Can disciples do that? Disciples have to walk their friends through restoration. We have to walk them through each of the eight steps. If we embrace the process, then we can take the promise in our mouth and God will honor it.

In Isaiah 55:6–9 we're encouraged to do that very thing:

> "Seek the LORD while He may be found, Call upon Him while He is near. Let the wicked forsake his way, And the unrighteous man his thoughts; Let him return to the LORD And He will have mercy on him; And to our God, For He will abundantly pardon. 'For My thoughts are not your thoughts, Nor are your ways My ways,' says the LORD. 'For as the heavens are higher than the earth, So are My ways higher than your ways, And My thoughts than your thoughts.'"

The promise is that when the individual returns to the Lord, God will have mercy on him and He will abundantly pardon—not sparsely pardon—but abundantly pardon! Abundant pardon has to have a demonstration from people. We have to supply the words and the hands of abundance. The touch of God has to come through the corporate church. God will certainly not allow us to extend it to the nation unless we faithfully extend it to each other. Nations desperately need the mercy of God. How do we qualify to extend it to a nation? We first have to extend it to each other in our natural and spiritual families.

Verses 10–13 of the same passage says:

> "For as the rain comes down, and the snow from heaven, And do not return there, But water the earth, And make it bring forth and

> bud, That it may give seed to the sower And bread to the eater, So shall My word be that goes forth from My mouth; It shall not return to Me void, But it shall accomplish what I please, And it shall prosper in the thing for which I send it. For you shall go out with joy, And be led out with peace; The mountains and the hills Shall break forth into singing before you, And all the trees of the field shall clap their hands. Instead of the thorn shall come up the cypress tree, And instead of the brier shall come up the myrtle tree; And it shall be to the LORD for a name, For an everlasting sign that shall not be cut off."

The only way we qualify to take the covenant of sure mercy and put it in our mouth is when we practice extending it to each other. God said He ordained this covenant to be spoken out of our mouth to a nation. We can confess it over our country when we're in prayer in the Throne Room. God says when we do, "It shall not return to Him void, but it shall accomplish what He pleases, and it shall prosper in the thing for which He sent it." When is the last time we confessed the covenant of sure mercy over our city, over our state, or over our nation? That is the call. A nation in judgment needs a people who can extend the covenant of sure mercy, forestalling the judgment and gaining a harvest. God will hold the church accountable for the condition of the land in the days ahead. It's time we grew up to be agents of restoration rather than agents of criticism and judgment. If we pay the price, God will honor our words!

IS HAVING HIS IMAGE
FORMED IN YOU
MORE IMPORTANT
THAN ALL ELSE YOU DO

HAVE YOUR PRIORITIES
BEEN SET STRAIGHT
IF SO, YOU HAVE CAUSE TO
CELEBRATE

Jayne Houghton

Footnotes

1. Richard Francis Weymouth, *The New Testament In Modern Speech,* Edited by Ernest Hampden-Cook, M.A., Third Edition 1911, p. 733. Re: Revelation 22:10–11, footnote #6, "Still."
2. *www.worldnetdaily.com/news/article.asp?ARTICLE_ID=38268,* posted April 30, 2004. *Law Of The Land,* "Bible as hate speech" signed into law.
3. *Lexical Aids to the New Testament* from Complete Word Study New Testament (1991 by AMG Int'l, Inc. 2nd Edition 1992), p. 892, Re: Acts 8:20–22.